Basic Knowledge
Higher Mathematics

I.S.B.N.   0 7169 3110 9

Basic Knowledge
Higher
Mathematics

J.F. MORGAN

ROBERT GIBSON · PUBLISHER
17, Fitzroy Place, Glasgow, G3 7SF

Author's Note

Notes, proofs, conventions, formulae, and numerous worked examples based on the syllabus for Higher Mathematics, are all grouped together in this reference book.

A comprehensive summary for revision, together with necessary methods and techniques, are described and explained. These, as well as native wit, are essential if the Higher Grade Examination is to be successfully attempted.

CONTENTS

Printed by ROBERT MACLEHOSE & Co., Ltd., *Glasgow, Scotland.*

ALGEBRA

Sequences and Series

Sequences

a)   1, 3, 5, 7, ...

b)   1, 1, 2, 3, 5, 8, ...

c)   2, 3, 5, 7, 11, ...

The above are all examples of sequences, some of which have
a simple formula for the nth term (Un) of the sequence, e.g.

a) $U_n = 2n - 1$. Some have a complicated formula for Un, e.g.

b) $U_n = \frac{1}{\sqrt{5}} \left(\frac{1 + \sqrt{5}}{2} \right)^n - \frac{1}{\sqrt{5}} \left(\frac{1 - \sqrt{5}}{2} \right)^n$, and again there
are some for which a formula has not yet been discovered, e.g.

c) the sequence of prime numbers.

A sequence maps the set of natural numbers (i.e. the domain) onto
the set of values of Un (i.e. the range) by means of a formula.

These mappings may be illustrated graphically.

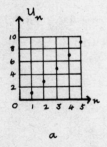

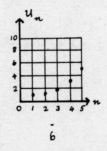

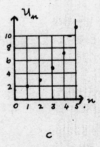

a

b

c

It should be noted that the mappings go in jumps, for it would make no
sense to join the points on the graph. Since the elements in the domain

are on the set N then there is no element between 2 and 3, say, with which to deal.

Series

When the terms of a sequence are added we refer to a series for which we may find the sum.

e.g. 1, 2, 3, 4, 5, 6, ... n is a sequence, but
1 + 2 + 3 + 4 + 5 + 6 + ...+n is a series.

Arithmetic Series

When there is a common difference between each pair of consecutive terms in a series then the series is an arithmetic one. The common difference in the above series is 1.

If we wish to add the first n terms of an arithmetic series then we say we are finding the sum to n terms (Sn, for short) of an arithmetic series i.e.

$Sn = 1 + 2 + 3 + 4$ . . . . $+ (n - 2) + (n - 1) + n$.

Writing this series backwards we have:

$Sn = n + (n - 1) + (n - 2) +$ . . . . $+ 4 + 3 + 2 + 1$.

By adding the two lines together we get:

$2\,Sn = (n + 1) + (n + 1) + (n + 1)$. . . .$+ (n + 1) + (n + 1) + (n + 1)$.

Giving n terms on the right-hand side, each of which is $(n + 1)$ i.e.
$n(n + 1)$. Now we have:

$2\,Sn = n(n + 1)$.

$\Leftrightarrow Sn = \dfrac{n}{2}(n + 1)$.

When the common difference is not 1, we may use the same system. Let us consider the general arithmetic series where the first term is a, the common difference is d, and the last term l.

8

$Sn = a + (a + d) + (a + 2d) \ldots\ldots\ldots\ldots\ldots + (l - 2d) + (l - d) + l.$

$Sn = l + (l - d) + (l - 2d) \ldots\ldots\ldots\ldots + (a + 2d) + (a + d) + a.$

By adding the two lines we get:

$2 Sn = (a + l) + (a + l) + (a + l) \ldots\ldots + (a + l) + (a + l) + (a + l).$

Giving n terms, each of which is $(a + l)$, and so.

$2 Sn = n (a + l)$

$\Leftrightarrow Sn = \dfrac{n (a + l)}{2}$ i.e. $Sn = n \times$ (the arithmetic mean of the first and last

terms).

By considering the last term, l, in terms of a and d we find $l = a + (n - 1)d$,
and we may rewrite the formula giving an alternative form.

$Sn = \dfrac{n}{2} (a + a + (n - 1) d)$

$= \dfrac{n}{2} [2a + (n - 1) d]$

Geometric Series

Another common series is the geometric, where there is a common ratio
between each pair of consecutive terms e.g. $2 + 4 + 8 \ldots\ldots\ldots + 2^n$.
Here the common ratio (r) is 2, because we have to multiply each term
by 2 to get the next, alternatively we may state this in a more mathe-
matical form as $\dfrac{Un}{Un-1} = 2$, i.e. the ratio of any term and the previous
term gives r, the common ratio, which in our example is 2.

The general form of a geometric series is $a + ar + ar^2 + ar^3 + \ldots\ldots + ar^{n-1}$
[N.B. there are n terms here].

The series may be written in two ways as before.

$Sn = a + ar + ar^2 + ar^3 \ldots\ldots\ldots\ldots\ldots\ldots + ar^{n-1}.$

Now we multiply both sides of the equation by r, the common ratio,
giving:

$r Sn = ar + ar^2 + ar^3 + ar^4 \ldots\ldots\ldots\ldots\ldots\ldots + ar^n.$

9

For convenience we will write the same two lines again but will realign them:

$$Sn = a + ar + ar^2 + ar^3 \ldots\ldots\ldots\ldots\ldots\ldots\ldots\ldots\ldots + ar^{n-1}$$

$$rSn = \quad ar + ar^2 + ar^3 \ldots\ldots\ldots\ldots\ldots\ldots\ldots\ldots\ldots + ar^{n-1} + ar^n$$

Now subtracting the second from the first:

$$Sn - rSn = a - ar^n$$

$$\Leftrightarrow (1 - r)\, Sn = a\,(1 - r^n)$$

$$\Leftrightarrow Sn = \frac{a\,(1 - r^n)}{1 - r}$$

[N.B. For this formula we cannot have r = 1, for then the denominator would be zero. In any case when the common ratio is 1 we are dealing with a series of the form $a + a + a \ldots\ldots\ldots\ldots + a$ to n terms, whose sum is simply na].

Sum to Infinity

Sometimes it is necessary to find the limit of a sum of an infinite number of terms of a geometric series i.e. $S\infty$

$$Sn = \frac{a\,(1 - r^n)}{1 - r} = \frac{a - ar^n}{1 - r} = \frac{a}{1 - r} - \frac{ar^n}{1 - r}$$

Now if $n \to \infty$ (n tends to an infinite value) and $|r| < 1$ i.e. $-1 < r < 1$

$$\frac{ar^n}{1 - r} \to \frac{0}{1 - r} \text{ leaving } S\infty = \frac{a}{1 - r} - \frac{0}{1 - r} = \frac{a}{1 - r}.$$

If $|r| > 1$ then $\dfrac{ar^n}{1 - r} \to \infty$ and so $S\infty$ does not tend to a definite value i.e. $S\infty$ does not have a limit which it will approach.

Limits

The following illustration gives some idea of what is meant by 'limits' in this context.

Consider a strip of paper 2 cm in length cut according to the following method.

Cut 1: 1 cm cut parallel to the sides   [Note 1 cm remains uncut]
Cut 2: ½ cm cut parallel to the sides   [Note ½ cm remains uncut]
Cut 3: ¼ cm cut parallel to the sides   [Note ¼ cm remains uncut]

Each successive cut must be of length ½ that of the previous cut.

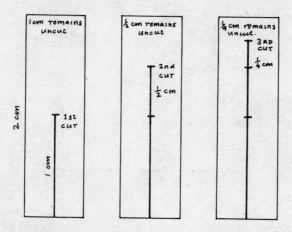

By adding the lengths of each cut as we go along we find the total length of the first 3 cuts to be:

$S_3 = 1 + \frac{1}{2} + \frac{1}{4}$ cm and $\frac{1}{4}$ cm remains uncut.

After 7 cuts:

$S_7 = 1 + \frac{1}{2} + \frac{1}{4} + \frac{1}{8} + \frac{1}{16} + \frac{1}{32} + \frac{1}{64}$ cm and $\frac{1}{64}$ cm remains uncut.

After n cuts:

$Sn = 1 + \frac{1}{2} + \frac{1}{4} + \frac{1}{8} \cdots + \frac{1}{2^{n-1}}$ cm and $\frac{1}{2^{n-1}}$ cm remains uncut.

By this method we will never succeed in cutting the strip into 2 separate pieces for even after an infinitely large number of cuts there will remain a very small amount uncut of equal length to the last cut made.

The total length of the cuts made will tend to 2 cm but will never quite be 2 cm. This 2 cm is the limit of the sum of the series of cuts i.e.

$S_\infty \to 2$.

The graph of the above series is illustrated below by mapping the number of terms onto the sum of the terms.

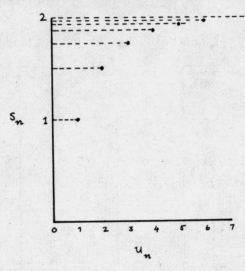

Examples

1. Find the sum to 8 terms of the series $5 + 7 + 9 + 11 \ldots \ldots$
   Here the common difference, d, is 2 so we have an arithmetic series.

   $$S_8 = \frac{8}{2} (2 \times 5 + (8 - 1)\, 2)$$
   $$= 4\, (10 + 14)$$
   $$= 96$$

2. Find the sum to 10 terms of the series $1 + \frac{1}{2} + \frac{1}{4} + \ldots \ldots$
   Here the common ratio is $\frac{1}{2}$ so we have a geometric series.

   $$S_{10} = \frac{1\,(1 - (\frac{1}{2})^{10})}{1 - \frac{1}{2}}$$
   $$= 2\, (1 - (\tfrac{1}{2})^{10})$$
   $$= 2 - (\tfrac{1}{2})^9$$

12

3. Find the sum to infinity of the series $1 + \frac{1}{3} + \frac{1}{9} + \ldots\ldots$, if it exists.

The common ratio is $\frac{1}{3}$ and since $-1 < \frac{1}{3} < 1$ the sum to infinity does exist.

Thus $S_\infty = \dfrac{1}{1 - \frac{1}{3}} = \frac{3}{2}$

4. Express $0.\overset{..}{4}\overset{}{5}$ as an equivalent common fraction.

Now $0.\overset{..}{4}\overset{}{5}$ means $0.\overset{}{4}54545 \ldots\ldots\ldots\ldots$

Written as a series this becomes:

$0.45 + 0.0045 + 0.000045 + \ldots\ldots\ldots$ which is a geometric series with common ratio $\frac{1}{100}$ and since $-1 < \frac{1}{100} < 1$ there is a sum to infinity. Thus:

$S_\infty = \dfrac{0.45}{1 - \frac{1}{100}} = \dfrac{0.45}{\frac{99}{100}} = \frac{45}{99} = \frac{5}{11}$

5. How many terms of the series $21 + 17 + 13 + 9 + \ldots\ldots\ldots$ are required to give the sum of 45?

Here we have an arithmetic series with common difference -4. We have to find the 'n' in the formula $Sn = \frac{n}{2}(2a + (n-1)d)$. We know $Sn = 45$, $a = 21$, $d = -4$, so by substitution:

$45 = \frac{n}{2}[2 \times 21 + (n-1)(-4)]$

$\Leftrightarrow \quad 90 = n\ (42 - 4n + 4)$

$\Leftrightarrow \quad 90 = 46n - 4n^2$

$\Leftrightarrow \quad 4n^2 - 46n + 90 = 0$

$\Leftrightarrow \quad 2n^2 - 23n + 45 = 0$

$\Leftrightarrow \quad (2n - 5)(n - 9) = 0$

$\Leftrightarrow \quad n = \frac{5}{2}$ or $n = 9$ So $n = 9$ since $n \in N$

Matrices

A matrix is a rectangular array of numbers to represent an ordered set from a given context.

The array is enclosed in brackets (   ) and each array is designated by a capital letter.

The number of rows, m (running horizontally) times the number of columns, n (running vertically) gives the order of a matrix. Where m = n we are dealing with a square matrix which has special properties.

Two matrices are equal when they are of the same order and their corresponding entries are equal.

$A = \begin{pmatrix} a & b \\ c & d \end{pmatrix}$ is a square matrix of order 2, and may represent the coefficients of x and y from 2 linear equations such as:

ax + by = 2

cx + dy = 3

A zero matrix, O, is one in which all the entries or elements are zero e.g. $\begin{pmatrix} o & o \\ o & o \end{pmatrix}$ and is the identity matrix for the addition of matrices.

e.g.   A + O = A = O + A

i.e. $\begin{pmatrix} a & b \\ c & d \end{pmatrix} + \begin{pmatrix} o & o \\ o & o \end{pmatrix} = \begin{pmatrix} a & b \\ c & d \end{pmatrix} = \begin{pmatrix} o & o \\ o & o \end{pmatrix} + \begin{pmatrix} a & b \\ c & d \end{pmatrix}$

A unit matrix I is one in which all the entries in the leading diagonal are 1 and all the other entries are zero.

e.g. $\begin{pmatrix} 1 & 0 \\ 0 & 1 \end{pmatrix}$ is the identity matrix for multiplication of square matrices of order 2.

e.g. AI = A = IA

i.e. $\begin{pmatrix} a & b \\ c & d \end{pmatrix} \begin{pmatrix} 1 & 0 \\ 0 & 1 \end{pmatrix} = \begin{pmatrix} a & b \\ c & d \end{pmatrix} = \begin{pmatrix} 1 & 0 \\ 0 & 1 \end{pmatrix} \begin{pmatrix} a & b \\ c & d \end{pmatrix}$

When two matrices are of the same order they are conformable for addition.

e.g. $A = \begin{pmatrix} a & b \\ c & d \end{pmatrix}, \qquad B = \begin{pmatrix} p & q \\ r & s \end{pmatrix}$

$$A + B = \begin{pmatrix} a & b \\ c & d \end{pmatrix} + \begin{pmatrix} p & q \\ r & s \end{pmatrix} = \begin{pmatrix} a+p & b+q \\ c+r & d+s \end{pmatrix}$$

Notice that the corresponding entries in each matrix are added and the result is another matrix of the same order as that of the original ones. When two matrices are of different orders their sum is not defined. The addition of matrices is commutative i.e. $A + B = B + A$.

The addition of matrices is associative i.e. $A + (B + C) = (A + B) + C$.

$A = \begin{pmatrix} a & b \\ c & d \end{pmatrix}$ has an additive inverse i.e.

$B = \begin{pmatrix} -a & -b \\ -c & -d \end{pmatrix}$ such that $A + B = O$.

This property allows the subtraction of matrices by adding the additive inverse.

e.g. $\begin{pmatrix} a & b \\ c & d \end{pmatrix} - \begin{pmatrix} p & q \\ r & s \end{pmatrix} = \begin{pmatrix} a & b \\ c & d \end{pmatrix} + \begin{pmatrix} -p & -q \\ -r & -s \end{pmatrix} = \begin{pmatrix} a-p & b-q \\ c-r & d-s \end{pmatrix}$

Notice that the difference is again of the same order as the two original matrices.

Matrices may be multiplied by a scalar number k, giving a product of the same order as the original matrix but with each element k times the original.

e.g. $k \begin{pmatrix} a & b \\ c & d \end{pmatrix} = \begin{pmatrix} ka & kb \\ kc & kd \end{pmatrix}$

Matrices may be multiplied if they are conformable for multiplication, i.e. when the number of columns in the first is equal to the number of rows in the second, e.g. an m x p matrix may premultiply a p x n matrix giving the product as an m x n matrix. By writing the orders of the matrices to be multiplied side by side in the order given we can check for conformability and learn the order of the product e.g.

m x (p   p) x n

If the middle numbers are the same then the matrices are conformable for multiplication and the product will be of order, the outer two numbers, m x n in our example.

In general, matrix multiplication is non commutative i.e. $AB \neq BA$ e.g. if A is of order m x p and B is of order p x n then the product AB is possible, but BA is not.

AB is m x (p   p) x n i.e. m x n
BA is p x n   m x p i.e. the middle numbers are not the same.

If $A = \begin{pmatrix} a & b \\ c & d \end{pmatrix}$ and $B = \begin{pmatrix} p & q \\ r & s \end{pmatrix}$ then

$$AB = \begin{pmatrix} ap + br & aq + bs \\ cp + dr & cq + ds \end{pmatrix}$$

Multiplication of matrices is associative i.e. $(AB)C = A(BC)$
Multiplication is distributive with respect to addition i.e.
$A(B + C) = AB + AC$.

Given $A = \begin{pmatrix} a & b \\ c & d \end{pmatrix}$ then $ad - bc$ is called the determinant of the matrix. If $ad - bc = o$ then the matrix is called singular i.e. it has no multiplicative inverse, A^{-1}.

All non-singular square matrices have a multiplicative inverse such that $A^{-1}A = I = AA^{-1}$ where A, A^{-1} and I are all of the same order.

The multiplicative inverse of a 2 x 2 matrix is formed by interchanging the elements in the leading diagonal, changing the sign of the elements in the other diagonal and dividing each element by the determinant.

e.g. $A = \begin{pmatrix} a & b \\ c & d \end{pmatrix}$ has a multiplicative inverse:

$$A^{-1} = \begin{pmatrix} \dfrac{d}{ad-bc} & \dfrac{-b}{ad-bc} \\ \dfrac{-c}{ad-bc} & \dfrac{a}{ad-bc} \end{pmatrix}$$

$$= \frac{1}{ad-bc} \begin{pmatrix} d & -b \\ -c & a \end{pmatrix}$$

Example

Solve for P which is a 2 x 2 matrix

$$P \begin{pmatrix} 1 & 2 \\ 3 & 4 \end{pmatrix} - \begin{pmatrix} 10 & 12 \\ 6 & 7 \end{pmatrix} = \begin{pmatrix} 1 & 4 \\ 1 & 5 \end{pmatrix}$$

$$P \begin{pmatrix} 1 & 2 \\ 3 & 4 \end{pmatrix} = \begin{pmatrix} 1 & 4 \\ 1 & 5 \end{pmatrix} + \begin{pmatrix} 10 & 12 \\ 6 & 7 \end{pmatrix}$$

$$= \begin{pmatrix} 11 & 16 \\ 7 & 12 \end{pmatrix}$$

$$P = \begin{pmatrix} 11 & 16 \\ 7 & 12 \end{pmatrix} \left[-\tfrac{1}{2} \begin{pmatrix} 4 & -2 \\ -3 & 1 \end{pmatrix} \right] \qquad \text{Note the order}$$

$$= -\tfrac{1}{2} \begin{pmatrix} 11 & 16 \\ 7 & 12 \end{pmatrix} \begin{pmatrix} 4 & -2 \\ -3 & 1 \end{pmatrix}$$

$$= -\tfrac{1}{2} \begin{pmatrix} -4 & -6 \\ -8 & -2 \end{pmatrix}$$

$$= \begin{pmatrix} 2 & 3 \\ 4 & 1 \end{pmatrix}$$

Example

Solve by matrix methods the system of equations

$$\begin{array}{ll} 2y + 7x = 9 \\ 3x + y = 4 \end{array} \quad \Leftrightarrow \quad \begin{array}{ll} 7x + 2y = 9 \\ 3x + y = 4 \end{array}$$

$$\Leftrightarrow \quad \begin{pmatrix} 7 & 2 \\ 3 & 1 \end{pmatrix} \begin{pmatrix} x \\ y \end{pmatrix} = \begin{pmatrix} 9 \\ 4 \end{pmatrix}$$

$$\Leftrightarrow \quad \begin{pmatrix} x \\ y \end{pmatrix} = \begin{pmatrix} 1 & -2 \\ -3 & 7 \end{pmatrix} \begin{pmatrix} 9 \\ 4 \end{pmatrix}$$

$$= \begin{pmatrix} 1 \\ 1 \end{pmatrix}$$

$$\Leftrightarrow \quad x = 1, \; y = 1$$

Transformation Matrices

Transformations such as reflections and rotations or dilatations can be performed by the use of matrices. The matrices which perform these transformations are found quite readily by considering what happens to two vertices of a unit square on a cartesian diagram.

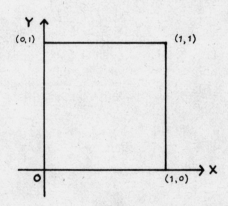

18

Under a reflection in the y-axis

$$\begin{pmatrix} 1 \\ 0 \end{pmatrix} \rightarrow \begin{pmatrix} -1 \\ 0 \end{pmatrix} \text{ and } \begin{pmatrix} 0 \\ 1 \end{pmatrix} \rightarrow \begin{pmatrix} 0 \\ 1 \end{pmatrix}$$

giving the transformation matrix

$$\begin{pmatrix} -1 & 0 \\ 0 & 1 \end{pmatrix}$$

Under a reflection in the x-axis

$$\begin{pmatrix} 1 \\ 0 \end{pmatrix} \rightarrow \begin{pmatrix} 1 \\ 0 \end{pmatrix} \text{ and } \begin{pmatrix} 0 \\ 1 \end{pmatrix} \rightarrow \begin{pmatrix} 0 \\ -1 \end{pmatrix}$$

giving $\begin{pmatrix} 1 & 0 \\ 0 & -1 \end{pmatrix}$

Under a reflection in the origin or under a rotation of 180° about the origin or under a dilatation [0, −1].

$$\begin{pmatrix} 1 \\ 0 \end{pmatrix} \rightarrow \begin{pmatrix} -1 \\ 0 \end{pmatrix} \text{ and } \begin{pmatrix} 0 \\ 1 \end{pmatrix} \rightarrow \begin{pmatrix} 0 \\ -1 \end{pmatrix}$$

giving $\begin{pmatrix} -1 & 0 \\ 0 & -1 \end{pmatrix}$ or $-1 \begin{pmatrix} 1 & 0 \\ 0 & 1 \end{pmatrix}$

The latter form leads to the interesting fact that a matrix which performs a dilatation [O, k] is of the form

$$\begin{pmatrix} k & 0 \\ 0 & k \end{pmatrix} \text{ or k } \begin{pmatrix} 1 & 0 \\ 0 & 1 \end{pmatrix}$$

Under a reflection in the line y = x

$$\begin{pmatrix} 1 \\ 0 \end{pmatrix} \rightarrow \begin{pmatrix} 0 \\ 1 \end{pmatrix} \text{ and } \begin{pmatrix} 0 \\ 1 \end{pmatrix} \rightarrow \begin{pmatrix} 1 \\ 0 \end{pmatrix}$$

giving $\begin{pmatrix} 0 & 1 \\ 1 & 0 \end{pmatrix}$

Under a rotation of 90° anticlockwise about the origin

$$\begin{pmatrix} 1 \\ 0 \end{pmatrix} \rightarrow \begin{pmatrix} 0 \\ 1 \end{pmatrix} \text{ and } \begin{pmatrix} 0 \\ 1 \end{pmatrix} \rightarrow \begin{pmatrix} -1 \\ 0 \end{pmatrix}$$

giving $\begin{pmatrix} 0 & -1 \\ 1 & 0 \end{pmatrix}$

Under a rotation of θ anticlockwise about the origin

$$\begin{pmatrix} 1 \\ 0 \end{pmatrix} \rightarrow \begin{pmatrix} \cos \theta \\ \sin \theta \end{pmatrix} \text{ and } \begin{pmatrix} 0 \\ 1 \end{pmatrix} \rightarrow \begin{pmatrix} -\sin \theta \\ \cos \theta \end{pmatrix}$$

giving $\begin{pmatrix} \cos \theta & -\sin \theta \\ \sin \theta & \cos \theta \end{pmatrix}$

Examples

a)   The image of the point (a, b) under a rotation of 90° anticlockwise about the origin is

$$\begin{pmatrix} 0 & -1 \\ 1 & 0 \end{pmatrix} \begin{pmatrix} a \\ b \end{pmatrix} = \begin{pmatrix} -b \\ a \end{pmatrix}$$

b)   The image of the point (a, b) under a rotation of 180° about the origin followed by a reflection in the line y = x is

$$\begin{pmatrix} 0 & 1 \\ 1 & 0 \end{pmatrix} \begin{pmatrix} -1 & 0 \\ 0 & -1 \end{pmatrix} \begin{pmatrix} a \\ b \end{pmatrix} \qquad \text{[Note the order]}$$

$$\Leftrightarrow \begin{pmatrix} 0 & -1 \\ -1 & 0 \end{pmatrix} \begin{pmatrix} a \\ b \end{pmatrix} = \begin{pmatrix} -b \\ -a \end{pmatrix}$$

Polynomials

A polynomial in one variable, x say, is an algebraic expression where the coefficients of the powers of x are not all zero and the powers are all elements of W.

Polynomials are said to be equal when they are of the same degree and their corresponding coefficients are equal.

The degree of a polynomial is the index of the highest power of the variable e.g. $5x^3 + 2x^2 + 4$ and $ax^3 + bx + c$ are both polynomials of degree 3. These two polynomials are equal when $a = 5$, $b = 2$ and $c = 4$.

The value of a polynomial can be found for any replacement of the variable e.g. the value of $5x^3 + 2x^2 + 4$ when $x = 2$ is $5(2)^3 + 2(2)^2 + 4 = 40 + 8 + 4 = 52$. However by rearranging the polynomial the value may be more efficiently calculated e.g. by nesting i.e.
$$(((5x + 2) x + 0) x + 4) = (((5.2 + 2) 2 + 0) 2 + 4) = 52.$$

Notice that '0' is inserted to fill the gap due to the absence of any term in 'x'.

This method can again be simplified for such evaluation by writing down only the coefficients of the variable in descending order of the degree of the variable.

e.g.

$$
\begin{array}{r|rrrr}
2 & 5 & 2 & 0 & 4 \\
 & & 5.2 & 12.2 & 24.2 \\
\hline
 & 5 & 12 & 24 & \underline{52}
\end{array}
\quad\Leftrightarrow\quad
\begin{array}{r|rrrr}
2 & 5 & 2 & 0 & 4 \\
 & & 10 & 24 & 48 \\
\hline
 & 5 & 12 & 24 & \underline{52}
\end{array}
$$

If the value of x in the general cubic polynomial, $ax^3 + bx^2 + cx + d$, is replaced by h then the value is calculated in the same way e.g.

$$
\begin{array}{r|rrrr}
h & a & b & c & d \\
 & & ah & ah^2 + bh & ah^3 + bh^2 + ch \\
\hline
 & a & ah + b & ah^2 + bh + c & \underline{ah^3 + bh^2 + ch + d}
\end{array}
$$

21

The value is then $ah^3 + bh^2 + ch + d$. We have replaced values before in solving equations e.g. $(x - 2)(5x + 2) = 0$ is a true statement when x is replaced by the value 2. This equation may be written in a more recognisable polynomial form as $5x^2 - 8x - 4 = 0$ using the above method

$$
\begin{array}{r|rrr}
2 & 5 & -8 & -4 \\
  &   & 10 & 4 \\
\hline
  & 5 & 2 & \underline{0}
\end{array}
$$

Notice we are left with the coefficient of the x and also the constant from the second bracket in the third line i.e. '5' and '2'. Also the third digit is '0' i.e. when $x - 2$ is a factor of the polynomial the third line gives the coefficients of the remaining factor, $(5x + 2)$. It only remains to discover the significance of the '0'.

In fact the '0' indicates that there is no remainder when the polynomial is divided by $x - 2$.

e.g. $\dfrac{(x - 2)(5x + 2) + 3}{x - 2} = \dfrac{5x^2 - 8x - 1}{x - 2}$

may be treated by long division as follows:

$$
\begin{array}{r}
5x + 2 \\
x - 2 \overline{\smash{)}\ 5x^2 - 8x - 1} \\
5x^2 - 10x \\
\hline
2x - 1 \\
2x - 4 \\
\hline
\text{Remainder} = 3
\end{array}
$$

OR

$$
\begin{array}{r|rrr}
2 & 5 & -8 & -1 \\
  &   & 10 & 4 \\
\hline
  & 5 & 2 & \underline{3} = \text{Remainder}
\end{array}
$$

by the quick method.

i.e. a polynomial $ax^3 + bx^2 + cx + d$ may be written in the form $(x - h)(ex^2 + fx + g) + R$ where $R = ah^3 + bh^2 + ch + d$ i.e. the remainder R may be found by the quick method after the division of a polynomial by a linear expression.

22

$$
\begin{array}{c|cccc}
h & a & b & c & d \\
  &   & ah & ah^2 + bh & ah^3 + bh^2 + ch \\
\hline
  & a & ah + b & ah^2 + bh + c & \underline{ah^3 + bh^2 + ch + d} \quad = \quad R
\end{array}
$$

Note that when the final expression in the last line of our quick method is zero in value then $x - h$ is a factor of the polynomial. If the final expression is not zero in value then $x - h$ is not a factor of the polynomial but the final value represents the remainder after division by $x - h$.

In general a polynomial $f(x) = (x - h)\,(Q(x)) + R$.

Summing up we can say that by use of the quick method above:

a) When $R = 0$ then $x - h$ is a factor of the polynomial.

b) When $R \neq 0$ then R represents the remainder on division of the polynomial by $x - h$.

c) R represents also the value of the polynomial when x is replaced by h.

Examples

a) Find the factors of $3x^3 + 4x^2 - 13x + 6$.

$$
\begin{array}{r|rrrr}
h = 1 & 3 & 4 & -13 & 6 \\
       &   & 3 & 7 & -6 \\
\cline{2-5}
h = -3 & 3 & 7 & -6 & \underline{0} \\
       &   & -9 & 6 & \\
\cline{2-5}
       & 3 & -2 & \underline{0} &
\end{array}
$$

$\Leftrightarrow$ $(x - 1)$ is a factor

$\Leftrightarrow$ $(x + 3)$ is a factor and $(3x - 2)$ is a factor.

Thus $3x^3 + 4x^2 - 13x + 6 \Leftrightarrow (x - 1)(x + 3)\,(3x - 2)$.

Notice how the above example makes use of the first quotient $(3x^2 + 7x - 6)$ to find the next factor.

23

b) Find the remainder on division of $3x^3 + 4x^2 - 13x + 7$ by $x - 1$.

$$
\begin{array}{r|rrrr}
1 & 3 & 4 & -13 & 7 \\
  &   & 3 & 7 & -6 \\
\hline
  & 3 & 7 & -6 & \underline{1} = R
\end{array}
$$

Remainder $= 1$

c) Evaluate $f(-3)$ when $f(x) = 3x^3 + 4x^2 - 13x + 8$

$$
\begin{array}{r|rrrr}
-3 & 3 & 4 & -13 & 8 \\
   &   & -9 & 15 & -6 \\
\hline
   & 3 & -5 & 2 & \underline{2} = f(-3)
\end{array}
$$

d) Show that $(3x - 2)$ is a factor of $3x^3 + 4x^2 - 13x + 6$. First change $(3x - 2)$ to the form $3(x - \frac{2}{3})$. Now show that $(x - \frac{2}{3})$ is a factor.

$$
\begin{array}{r|rrrr}
\frac{2}{3} & 3 & 4 & -13 & 6 \\
   &   & 2 & 4 & -6 \\
\hline
   & 3 & 6 & -9 & \underline{0}
\end{array}
$$
$\Leftrightarrow$ $(x - \frac{2}{3})$ is a factor.

Now $3x^3 + 4x^2 - 13x + 6 = (x - \frac{2}{3})(3x^2 + 6x - 9)$.

If we now multiply the first factor by 3 giving $(3x - 2)$ we must divide the second factor by 3 giving $(x^2 + 2x - 3)$, thus the factors are $(3x - 2)(x^2 + 2x - 3)$ $\Leftrightarrow$ $(3x - 2)(x - 1)(x + 3)$.

e) Find the value of k for which $x^3 - 3x^2 + kx + 6$ has a factor $(x + 3)$.

$$
\begin{array}{r|rrrr}
-3 & 1 & -3 & k & 6 \\
   &   & -3 & 18 & -3k - 54 \\
\hline
   & 1 & -6 & 18 + k & \underline{-3k - 48} = R
\end{array}
$$

If $(x + 3)$ is a factor then $R = -3k - 48 = 0$

$\Leftrightarrow$ $\quad 3k = -48$

$\Leftrightarrow$ $\quad k = -16$

24

Quadratic Equations and Functions

$ax^2 + bx + c$ is a quadratic expression.

$ax^2 + bx + c = 0$ is a quadratic equation.

If a, b, c are real then the expression and the equation are said to be real.

If a, b, c are rational then the expression and the equation are said to be rational.

Although the coefficients of an equation are real and rational the roots i.e. the solution set need not be so.

The nature of the roots is determined by using the discriminant i.e. $b^2 - 4ac$, which comes from the formula for finding the roots of a quadratic equation i.e.

$$x = \frac{-b \pm \sqrt{b^2 - 4ac}}{2a}$$

1. If $b^2 - 4ac = 0$ the roots are $\dfrac{-b + 0}{2a}$ and $\dfrac{-b - 0}{2a}$ i.e. both roots are co-incident at $\dfrac{-b}{2a}$. Such a condition arises when the graph of the function is as in the figure below.

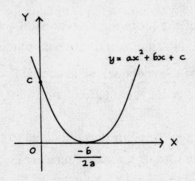

25

In this figure the roots are shown to be identical when the x-axis is a tangent at the point on the curve where $x = \dfrac{-b}{2a}$.

The nature of the roots depends on the nature of $\dfrac{-b}{2a}$ and the equation or expression will be of the same nature.

2. If $b^2 - 4ac > 0$ the roots are $\dfrac{-b + \sqrt{b^2 - 4ac}}{2a}$ and $\dfrac{-b - \sqrt{b^2 - 4ac}}{2a}$. Such a condition arises when the graph of the function is as in the figure below.

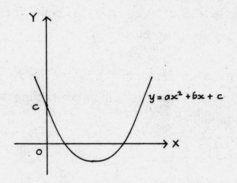

In this figure the roots are the values of x where the curve cuts the x-axis.

i) The nature of the roots will be rational if a and b are rational and $b^2 - 4ac$ is a square of a rational number.

ii) The nature of the roots will be irrational if a or b are irrational or if $b^2 - 4ac$ is not the square of a rational number.

3. If $b^2 - 4ac < 0$ then the roots do not belong to the set of real numbers, since the root of a negative number i.e. $b^2 - 4ac < 0$ is not a real number. Such a condition arises when the graph of the

function is as in the figure below.

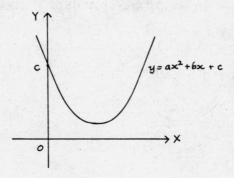

In this figure the graph does not cut the x-axis and so the equation it represents has no real roots. By testing the discriminant, $b^2 - 4ac$, the nature of the factors of $f(x) = ax^2 + bx + c$ are determined. When the condition illustrated in 3 above arises we say the expression is irreducible i.e. when no real factors exist.

All the diagrams shown have assumed that 'a', the coefficient of x^2, is positive. If 'a' is negative then the graphs of the functions will have maximum turning values and the graphs would appear reflected in the x-axis but all the information gathered would stand as before.

Relation between Roots and Coefficients

If α is a root of $ax^2 + bx + c = 0$ then $(x - \alpha)$ is a factor of $ax^2 + bx + c$.
If β is a root of $ax^2 + bx + c = 0$ then $(x - \beta)$ is a factor of $ax^2 + bx + c$.
Also $(x - \alpha)(x - \beta) = x^2 - (\alpha + \beta)x + \alpha\beta$
Therefore $a(x - \alpha)(x - \beta) = a[x^2 - (\alpha + \beta)x + \alpha\beta] = ax^2 + bx + c$.
Thus $\alpha + \beta = \dfrac{-b}{a}$ and $\alpha\beta = \dfrac{c}{a}$ because the corresponding coefficients of equal polynomials are equal to each other.

Examples

i) Find p and q when α and β are the roots of $x^2 - px + q = 0$.

$$(x - \alpha)(x - \beta) = x^2 - (\alpha + \beta)x + \alpha\beta$$
$$= x^2 - px + q$$
$$\Leftrightarrow p = \alpha + \beta \text{ and } q = \alpha\beta$$

ii) Find $\dfrac{1}{\alpha} + \dfrac{1}{\beta}$ in terms of p and q.

$$p = \alpha + \beta, \quad q = \alpha\beta$$

$$\frac{1}{\alpha} + \frac{1}{\beta} = \frac{\beta + \alpha}{\alpha\beta} = \frac{p}{q}$$

iii) Find $\alpha^2 + \alpha\beta + \beta^2$ in terms of p and q.

$$\alpha^2 + \alpha\beta + \beta^2 = (\alpha^2 + 2\alpha\beta + \beta^2) - \alpha\beta$$
$$= (\alpha + \beta)^2 - \alpha\beta$$
$$= p^2 - q.$$

Irrationals of form $p \pm \sqrt{q}$

Because the formula for solving the quadratic equation is of the form

$$x = \frac{-b \pm \sqrt{b^2 - 4ac}}{2a}$$

$$= \frac{-b}{2a} + \frac{\sqrt{b^2 - 4ac}}{2a} \quad \text{or} \quad \frac{-b}{2a} - \frac{\sqrt{b^2 - 4ac}}{2a}$$

$$= p + \sqrt{q} \quad \text{or} \quad p - \sqrt{q}$$

then given one root of a quadratic equation it is clear what the other root must be. For example if $2 + \sqrt{3}$ is a root of a quadratic equation then $2 - \sqrt{3}$ is the other root.

Irrational numbers which differ only in the sign between the first and second terms are called conjugates of each other.

Thus $2 + \sqrt{3}$ is the conjugate of $2 - \sqrt{3}$ and vice versa.

28

Rationalising the denominator $p \pm \sqrt{q}$

The evaluation of the form $\dfrac{r}{p+\sqrt{q}}$ or $\dfrac{r}{p-\sqrt{q}}$ can be awkward, but the following method simplifies the working.

Example

Evaluate $\dfrac{7}{3-\sqrt{2}}$ correct to 3 decimal places.

First find the conjugate of the denominator i.e. $3+\sqrt{2}$. Now multiply the numerator and the denominator by it i.e.

$$\frac{7}{3-\sqrt{2}} \quad \frac{3+\sqrt{2}}{3+\sqrt{2}} \quad = \quad \frac{7(3+\sqrt{2})}{9-2}$$

$$= \quad \frac{7(3+\sqrt{2})}{7}$$

$$= \quad 3 + \sqrt{2}$$

$$= \quad 3 + 1.414$$

$$= \quad 4.414 \text{ to } 3 \text{ d.p's}$$

Composition of Functions and Inverses

A function is the mapping of a set A, called the domain, onto a set B, called the range, such that for every element in A there is one and only one corresponding image in B. In symbols, if $a \in A$ then $f(a) \in B$.

When only a few elements are involved in each set we may represent the function or mapping by a list of ordered pairs where the first element is from the set A and the second element is from the set B.

e.g. (1, 2) (2, 4) (3, 6) (4, 8)

or by an arrow diagram such as:

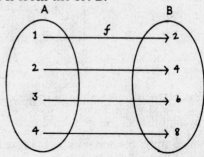

or on a cartesian diagram

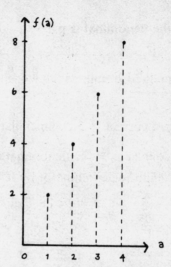

These forms represent the function f, where 'f' means 'multiply the element of A by 2 to find f(a).'

When we wish to illustrate the general function f we may use the set builder notation $\{(x, y): y = 2x, x, y \in R\}$.

Note that 'f' is a rule or formula to describe how the element of the range is to be established.

Notice that each and every element of the domain, A, must have an image in the range, B, but not all the elements in B need be images e.g.

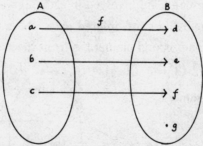

When all the elements of B are images then a one-to-one correspondence is established and gives rise to an inverse function i.e. a mapping of the set B onto the set A. This inverse mapping is denoted by f^{-1}.   e.g.

30

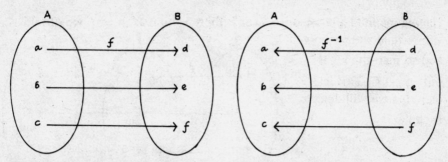

Notice that when a function has an inverse then the domain, A becomes the range and the range B becomes the domain for f^{-1}.

The inverse of a function is also a function and must obey the rules of a function.

The inverse of a function is NOT the same as the inverse of a matrix. The graphs of a function and its inverse are images of each other under reflection in the line y = x.

e.g.   The diagram below illustrates the inverse of f(x) = 2x + 4 i.e.
$f^{-1}(x)$ = ½x − 2.

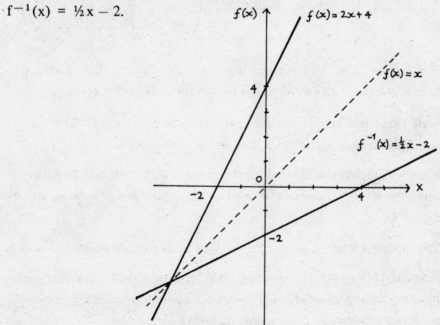

Having mapped a set A onto a set B there is no reason why we should not extend the process and so map the set B onto a set C. This last mapping we will denote by g i.e.

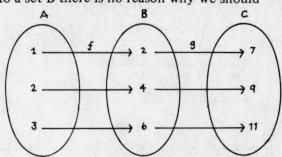

Here 'f' means 'multiply each element of A by 2', and 'g' means 'add 5 to each element of B'.

By omitting the middle step we could describe a function or mapping h which maps the set A onto the set C.

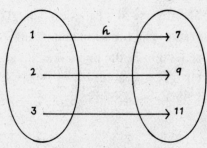

Here $h(x) = 2x + 5$ or if we describe the whole process step by step $h(x) = g \circ f$ (read g circle f) or $h(x) = (g \circ f)(x)$ or $h(x) = g(f(x))$.

Note that the order is the same as the original steps i.e. f first then g, which means multiply x by 2 then add 5 to the result.

What we are doing here is taking the range of A, which is B, and then using the set B as a domain from which we establish a new range, namely the set C.

The function h which goes from set A to set C is a composite of g and f.

In general if f and g are functions with domains A (for f) and B (for g) then the composition of functions $g \circ f$ is a new function, $h(x)$ where the domain of $h(x) = \{ x: \ x \in A, \ f(x) \in B \}$.

Inverse of a Composite Function

The inverse of a composite function $g \circ f$ is $(g \circ f)^{-1}$ and is found by a step by step method.

First note that $(g \circ f)^{-1} = f^{-1} \circ g^{-1}$

$\qquad f^{-1} \circ g^{-1}$

$\Leftrightarrow \quad (f^{-1} \circ g^{-1}) \circ I$

$\Leftrightarrow \quad (f^{-1} \circ g^{-1}) \circ [(g \circ f) \circ (g \circ f)^{-1}]$

$\Leftrightarrow \quad (f^{-1} \circ (g^{-1} \circ g) \circ f) \circ (g \circ f)^{-1} \quad$ by the associative law

$\Leftrightarrow \quad (f^{-1} \circ I \circ f) \circ (g \circ f)^{-1}$

$\Leftrightarrow \quad (f^{-1} \circ f) \circ (g \circ f)^{-1}$

$\Leftrightarrow \quad I \circ (g \circ f)^{-1}$

$\Leftrightarrow \quad (g \circ f)^{-1}$

Let $h(x) = 2x + 3$ where $h(x) = (g \circ f)(x)$
$f(x)$ means multiply x by 2, then
$f^{-1}(x)$ means divide x by 2.
$g(x)$ means add 3 to the result, then
$g^{-1}(x)$ means subtract 3 from the result.

Now $f^{-1} \circ g^{-1}$ means first subtract 3 from x then divide the result by 2 i.e. $(g \circ f)^{-1}(x) = \dfrac{(x-3)}{2}$.

A quick method of finding the inverse of a composite function e.g. $f(x) = 2x + 3$ is to change the subject of the formula to x i.e.

$x = \dfrac{f(x)-3}{2}$ then replace $f(x)$ by x and the x by $f^{-1}(x)$, giving

$f^{-1}(x) = \dfrac{x-3}{2}$ as before.

Note that the inverse of reciprocating is also reciprocating e.g.

B

$$f(x) = \frac{x-2}{x} \quad \text{i.e. take the reciprocal of } x$$

$$= 1 - \frac{2}{x} \quad \text{multiply by } -2 \text{ and add 1 to the result.}$$

$$f^{-1}(x) = \frac{-2}{x-1} \quad \text{i.e. subtract 1 from x then divide by } -2 \text{ and take the reciprocal of the result.}$$

$$= \frac{2}{1-x}$$

Examples

1) Find a formula for a) f o g: b) g o f where $f(x) = 2x - 1$, $g(x) = x^2 - 1$ $x \in R$.

Find also, if it exists c) $g^{-1}(x)$, d) $f^{-1}(x)$, e) $g \circ f(3)$.

a) $(f o g)(x) = f(x^2 - 1) = 2(x^2 - 1) - 1 = 2x^2 - 3$

b) $(g o f)(x) = g(2x - 1) = (2x - 1)^2 - 1 = 4x(x - 1)$

c) $g^{-1}(x) \neq \pm\sqrt{x + 1}$ Since two results are possible there is no $1 - 1$ correspondence so no inverse exists.

d) $f^{-1}(x) = \frac{x+1}{2}$

e) $(g o f)(3) = 4.3(3 - 1) = 24$

Systems of Equations

Linear equations in 2 variables were dealt with in 'O' level maths. Here we will employ a method of solution using matrices.

Solve $\quad 2x + 3y = 8$
$$x + 2y = 5$$

The equations above may be represented by AX = B.

i.e. $\begin{pmatrix} 2 & 3 \\ 1 & 2 \end{pmatrix} \begin{pmatrix} x \\ y \end{pmatrix} = \begin{pmatrix} 8 \\ 5 \end{pmatrix}$

Let $A = \begin{pmatrix} 2 & 3 \\ 1 & 2 \end{pmatrix}$, $\qquad X = \begin{pmatrix} x \\ y \end{pmatrix}$, $\qquad B = \begin{pmatrix} 8 \\ 5 \end{pmatrix}$

Now by matrix algebra

$$AX = B$$

$$\Leftrightarrow \quad A^{-1}AX = A^{-1}B$$

$$\Leftrightarrow \quad IX = A^{-1}B$$

$$\Leftrightarrow \quad X = A^{-1}B$$

$$A^{-1} \quad = \quad \frac{1}{4-3}\begin{pmatrix} 2 & -3 \\ -1 & 2 \end{pmatrix}$$

$$= \begin{pmatrix} 2 & -3 \\ -1 & 2 \end{pmatrix}$$

$$A^{-1}B \quad = \quad \begin{pmatrix} 2 & -3 \\ -1 & 2 \end{pmatrix}\begin{pmatrix} 8 \\ 5 \end{pmatrix} = \begin{pmatrix} 1 \\ 2 \end{pmatrix} = \quad X$$

$$\text{i.e.} \begin{pmatrix} x \\ y \end{pmatrix} = \begin{pmatrix} 1 \\ 2 \end{pmatrix}$$

$$S.S. = \{(1, 2)\}$$

Systems of Equations in Three Variables

The above method is not so convenient when three variables are involved since the calculation of the inverse of a 3 x 3 matrix is more complex. However the method of elimination is simple to adopt for systems of equations in three variables.

Example

Solve:
$$2x + y - z = 2 \quad \text{_____ (A)}$$
$$x + 2y + 2z = 10 \quad \text{_____ (B)}$$
$$3x - 3y + z = 6 \quad \text{_____ (C)}$$

By taking two pairs of equations from the three above we eliminate one variable at a time.

We will start by eliminating z from equations (A) and (C) by adding them.

i.e. $(2x + y - z) + (3x - 3y + z) = 2 + 6.$

$\Leftrightarrow \quad 5x - 2y = 8$ ———————————————— (D)

Similarly we eliminate the same variable, z, from (A) and (B) by multiplying (A) by 2 and adding it to (B).

i.e. $2(2x + y - z) + (x + 2y + 2z) \quad = \quad 4 + 10$

$\Leftrightarrow \quad 4x + 2y - 2z + x + 2y + 2z \quad = \quad 14$

$\Leftrightarrow \quad 5x + 4y \quad = \quad 14$ ———————————— (E)

Now by taking our two new equations in two variables, i.e. equations (D) and (E), we have a familiar system to deal with.

Subtract (D) from (E) to eliminate x.

i.e. $(5x + 4y) - (5x - 2y) = 14 - 8$

$\Leftrightarrow \quad 4y + 2y = 6$

$\Leftrightarrow \quad 6y \quad = 6$

$\Leftrightarrow \quad y \quad = 1$

By substitution in (D)

$5x - 2(1) \quad = \quad 8$

$\Leftrightarrow \quad 5x \quad = \quad 10$

$\Leftrightarrow \quad x \quad = \quad 2$

By substitution in (A)

$2(2) + 1 - z = 2$

$\Leftrightarrow \quad 5 - z \quad = 2$

$\Leftrightarrow \quad z \quad = 3$

Hence SS $= \{(2, 1, 3)\}$

Exponential & Logarithmic Functions

The mapping $f : x \rightarrow a^x$ where $a > 0$ and $a \neq 1$, and $x \in R$, defines the exponential function with base a.

The graph of the exponential function is shown below (for $a > 1$).

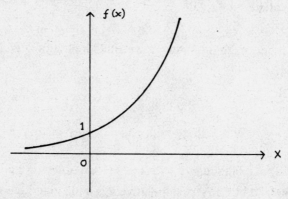

The graph of the inverse of this function will be the reflection of the above graph in the line $f(x) = x$. This inverse is the graph of the logarithmic function and is shown below.

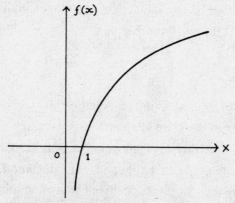

The inverse of $f(x) = a^x$ is $f^{-1}(x) = \log_a x$ (log x to the base a) e.g. the inverse of 10^2 is $\log_{10} 2$ (log 2 to the base 10).

The laws of logarithms are easily recalled if we remember how we have been using the log tables to make our calculations e.g. to multiply two numbers p and q, say, we find the log p and log q then add i.e.

$$\log pq = \log p + \log q \dots\dots\dots\dots\dots\dots\dots\dots 1$$

To divide one number, p, by another, q, we find their logs and subtract one from the other i.e.

$$\log \frac{p}{q} = \log p - \log q \dots\dots\dots\dots\dots\dots\dots\dots 2$$

To raise a number, p, to a power, n, we find the log of p and multiply it by n i.e.

$$\log p^n = n \log p \dots\dots\dots\dots\dots\dots\dots\dots\dots 3$$

$$\log_a a = 1 \dots\dots\dots\dots\dots\dots\dots\dots\dots\dots\dots 4$$

$$\log_a 1 = 0 \dots\dots\dots\dots\dots\dots\dots\dots\dots\dots\dots 5 \quad \text{for any base a.}$$

These laws we have been using with our calculations have all been with logs to the base 10 but any base positive a, $a \neq 1$, may be employed. The two most common bases for logs are 10 and e (2.72) and when the base is obvious we do not have to indicate it in our notation. Some calculations are performed invariably in base e and so it may be necessary to use our log tables in base 10 to evaluate the result. A simple law will convert logs of one base to those of another viz:

$$\log_a x = \frac{\log_{10} x}{\log_{10} a}$$

The base e is useful in calculations involving natural growth or decay as occurs in plants or radioactive elements. This law is of the form $A_t = A_0 e^{kt}$ where A_0 stands for a value at a chosen origin in time and A_t for the value at another time, e is the constant 2.72, t again is the other time and k a constant, positive for growth, negative for decay.

e.g. A radioactive element decays at a rate given by $M_t = M_0 e^{-kt}$ where M_0 is the initial mass and M_t is the mass after t years. If $M_0 = 50$gm find the half life of the element given $k = 0.05$. The half life occurs when the mass is half the original i.e. when $M_t = \frac{1}{2} M_0$.

38

Since $M_t = M_0 e^{-0.05t}$

$\Leftrightarrow \quad \frac{1}{2}M_0 = M_0 e^{-0.05t}$

$\Leftrightarrow \quad \frac{1}{2} = e^{-0.05t}$

$\Leftrightarrow \quad \log 0.5 = \log(e^{-0.05t})$

$\Leftrightarrow \quad \log 0.5 = -0.05t \; \log e$

$\Leftrightarrow \quad t = \dfrac{\log 0.5}{-0.05 \log e}$

[Note how base e would be convenient here since $\log_e e = 1$].

$\Leftrightarrow \quad t = \dfrac{\overline{1}.699}{(-0.05)(0.435)}$

$\qquad = \dfrac{-1 + 0.699}{(-0.05)(0.435)}$

$\qquad = \dfrac{-0.301}{(-0.05)(0.435)}$

$\qquad = \dfrac{0.301}{(0.05)(0.435)}$

$\qquad = 13.9$

no	log
0.05	$\overline{2}.699$
0.435	$\overline{1}.638$
	$\overline{2}.337$
0.301	$\overline{1}.479$
	$\overline{2}.337$
	1.142

The half life occurs then after 13.9 yr.

Examples:

a) Find x when $\log_x 49 = 2$

$\qquad \log_x 49 = 2$

$\Leftrightarrow \quad x^2 = 49$

$\Leftrightarrow \quad x = 7 \qquad$ Remember $x > 0$

b) Find x when $\log_{1/4} 64 = x$

$\qquad \log_{1/4} 64 = x$

$\Leftrightarrow \quad (\frac{1}{4})^x = 64$

$\Leftrightarrow \quad (\frac{1}{4})^x = 4^3$

$\Leftrightarrow \quad (\frac{1}{4})^x = (\frac{1}{4})^{-3}$

$\Leftrightarrow \quad x = -3$

c) Solve $\log_5 (3-2x) + \log_5 (2+x) = 1$. $x \in R$.

$$\log_5 (3-2x) + \log_5 (2+x) = \log_5 (3-2x)(2+x)$$
$$= \log_5 (6-x-2x^2)$$

$\Leftrightarrow \quad \log_5 (6-x-2x^2) = 1$

$\Leftrightarrow \quad 6-x-2x^2 = 5^1$

$\Leftrightarrow \quad 2x^2 + x - 1 = 0$

$\Leftrightarrow \quad (2x-1)(x+1) = 0$

$\Leftrightarrow \quad x = \frac{1}{2} \qquad x = -1$

The Form $y = ax^n$

If x and y are two variables connected by the law $y = ax^n$ then by the laws of logs.

$$\log y = \log a + \log x^n$$
$$= \log a + n \log x$$
$$= n \log x + \log a$$

By the substitution $Y = \log y$, $X = \log x$ and $c = \log a$ the above equation may be written in the form $Y = nX + c$ which is the form of an equation of a straight line.

In general the graph of log y against log x is a straight line $\Leftrightarrow y = ax^n$.

Example:

Corresponding readings of x and y in an experiment are given in the table.

x	1.0	1.5	2.0	3.0	4.0
y	2.50	8.42	20.0	67.5	160

Show that $y = ax^n$ and find 'a' and 'n'.

40

Using log tables we convert the above to:

$\log_{10} x$	0	0.176	0.301	0.477	0.602
$\log_{10} y$	0.398	0.925	1.301	1.829	2.204

Plotting $\log_{10} x$ against $\log_{10} y$ and drawing the best fitting straight line through these points we have the diagram below.

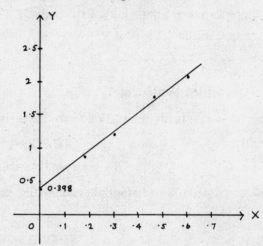

Now $y = ax^n \Leftrightarrow \log y = n \log x + \log a$

$$\Leftrightarrow \quad Y = nX + c$$

Here $c = \log a = 0.4 \Leftrightarrow a = 2.5$

From the graph we choose the points $(0.53, 2)$ and $(0.2, 1)$.

Thus $n = \dfrac{2-1}{0.53-0.2} = \dfrac{1}{0.33} \doteq 3$

Deductive Reasoning

Negation

If p is a statement then $\sim$ p ('not p') is the denial of this statement. If one is true then the other is false i.e. p and $\sim$ p have opposite truth values.

41

e.g. if p is the statement "today is Friday"
  ~p is the statement "today is not Friday".

Quantified Sentences

A quantified sentence tells how many elements of a given set are referred to. Such sentences will contain the word "all" or "every" or "each" which words are universal quantifiers. Alternatively the word "some" may appear which means 'at least one' and is called the existential quantifier.

Negation of Quantified Sentences

The negation of a universally quantified sentence is formed as below.

STATEMENT P	NEGATION ~ P
All P's are Q's	Some P's are **not** Q's

Similarly the negation of an existentially quantified sentence is formed as below.

STATEMENT P	NEGATION ~ P
Some P's are Q's	All P's are **not** Q's

The Converse

If $p \Rightarrow q$ is a given implication the converse is the form $q \Rightarrow p$.

If an implication is true its converse need not be so and vice versa. If both the implication and its converse are true then we have an equivalence $p \Leftrightarrow q$.

The Contrapositive

If $p \Rightarrow q$ is a given implication the contrapositive is the form $\sim q \Rightarrow \sim p$ and is equivalent to $p \Rightarrow q$. Thus if the implication is true so also is its contrapositive and vice versa.

Statements in mathematics may be linked together by implication ($\Rightarrow$), equivalence ($\Leftrightarrow$), conjunction ($\wedge$, and), disjunction ($\vee$, inclusive or) or denied by negation ($\sim$). By thus linking statements together we may prove a required result by deductive reasoning i.e. by working from the truth of one or more already known statements to a combination or single statement whose truth has not been known. Such a proof is by direct deductive reasoning.

Alternatively a combination of single statements may be proved indirectly by showing that any alternative is unacceptable.

It is important to distinguish between what is logically valid and what we would call 'true' e.g.

> "If 2 is an even number it is not prime".
> "2 is an even number".
> "2 is not prime".

This argument is valid even though its conclusion is certainly not true. The validity of the logical structure is independent of the truth of the statements involved. In the above argument the first implication is in fact false because by writing it in the form $p \Rightarrow q$ the statement p is true, but q is not, since it stands for "2 is not prime". The use of the word ' it ' instead of '2' disguised this fact.

GEOMETRY

Composite Transformations

To reflect in any number of parallel axes we need only learn how to find the image of a point under reflection in one axis, for all other reflections are similarly performed one after another.

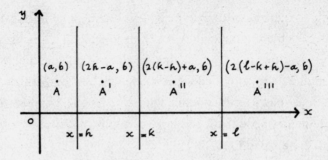

The image of A'(a, b) under reflection in the line x = h is A' (2h − a, b).

The image of A' (2h − a, b) under reflection in the line x = k is A''
(2k − (2h − a), b) i.e. (2(k − h) + a, b).

The image of A'' (2(k − h) + a, b) under reflection in the line x = l is A'''
(2l − [2(k − h) + a], b) i.e. (2(l − k + h) − a, b).

Notice that an even number of axes of reflection gives a result which is
equivalent to a translation parallel to the x-axis, but an odd number of
reflections gives the equivalent of a reflection in a line parallel to the
y-axis.

A reflection in two intersecting axes is equivalent to a rotation of twice
the angle between the two axes.

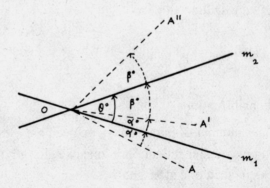

Let M_1 represent the reflection in the first axis and M_2 represent the reflection in the second axis, and $R_2\theta$ represent a rotation of $2\theta°$ about the intersection of the axes in the direction of first axis of reflection to the second. Algebraically.

$R_2\theta = M_2 \circ M_1$ [Note the order].

By constructing a composition of transformations

i) $M_2 \circ R_2\theta = M_2 \circ (M_2 \circ M_1)$
$= (M_2 \circ M_2) \circ M_1$
$= I \circ M_1$
$= M_1.$

ii) $R_2\theta \circ M_1 = (M_2 \circ M_1) \circ M_1$
$= M_2 \circ (M_1 \circ M_1)$
$= M_2 \circ I$
$= M_2$

Here we find that i) a rotation of $2\theta°$ followed by a reflection is equivalent to a reflection in a line making an angle $-\theta°$ with the first axis of reflection: ii) a reflection in a line followed by a rotation of $2\theta°$ is equivalent to a reflection in an axis which makes an angle of $\theta°$ with the first axis of reflection.

This is all we need to know in order to reflect in any number of concurrent axes e.g.

$M_3 \circ M_2 \circ M_1 = M_3 \circ R_2\theta$, where the angle between m_2 and m_1 is $\theta°$.

Now $M_3 \circ R_2\theta = M$, where M is a reflection in a line making an angle $-\theta°$ with m_3.

Similarly $M_4 \circ M_3 \circ M_2 \circ M_1 = R_2\phi \circ R_2\theta$
$= R_2(\phi + \theta)$

where $\phi°$ is the angle between m_4 and m_3, and $\theta°$ is the angle between m_2 and m_1.

45

Notice that reflection in an even number of axes is equivalent to a rotation and that a reflection in an odd number of axes is equivalent to a reflection.

Equations of lines under transformations

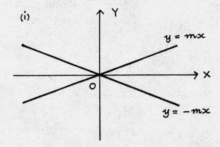

Under reflection in the y-axis the equation of the image of the line $y = mx$ is $y = -mx$.

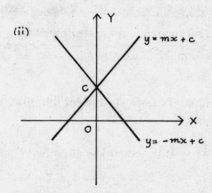

Under reflection in the y-axis the equation of the image of the line $y = mx + c$ is $y = -mx + c$.

The rule then is to change only the sign of the gradient under reflection in the y-axis.

(iii)

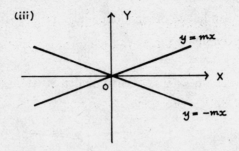

Under reflection in the x-axis the equation of the image of the line
y = mx is y = − mx.

(iv)

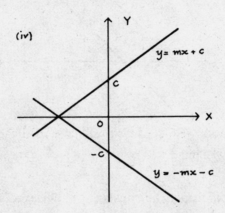

Under reflection in the x-axis the equation of the image of the line
y = mx + c is y = −mx − c.

The rule is to change the sign of both the gradient and the constant
under reflection in the x-axis.

(v)

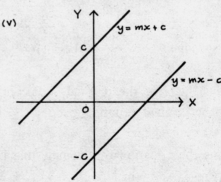

Under reflection in the origin the equation of the image of the line
y = mx + c is y = mx − c.

The rule is to change only the sign of the constant.

vi)

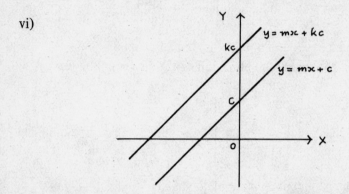

Under a dilatation [O, k] the equation of the image of the line
y = mx + c is y = mx + kc.

The rule is to multiply the constant by the scale factor of the dilatation.

Some transformations are more complex e.g. find the equation of the
image of the line y = mx + c where (a, b), which is on the line, is mapped
onto (2a − 1, 2b + 3).

a^1 = 2a − 1   ⟺   a = ½(a^1 + 1)
b^1 = 2b + 3   ⟺   b = ½(b^1 − 3)

Thus the x of the original equation becomes ½ (X + 1) and the y
of the original equation becomes ½ (Y − 3).

Thus the equation of the new line i.e. the image of y = mx + c is
½ (Y − 3) = m [½ (X + 1)] + c.

Gradient of a line from two given points

Given $A(x_A, y_A)$ and $B(x_B, y_B)$ then the gradient of AB is given by

$$\frac{y_B - y_A}{x_B - x_A}.$$

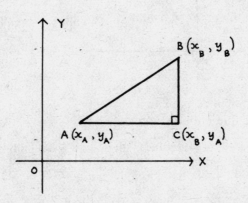

From the diagram the gradient of AB is given by $\dfrac{BC}{AC} = \dfrac{y_B - y_A}{x_B - x_A}$

Example

Find the gradient of the join between the points $A(3,4)$, $B(5,7)$. By substitution in the formula.

$$M_{AB} = \frac{y_B - y_A}{x_B - x_A}$$

$$= \frac{7 - 4}{5 - 3}$$

$$= \frac{3}{2}$$

The equation $y = mx$ of the line L through the origin with gradient m.

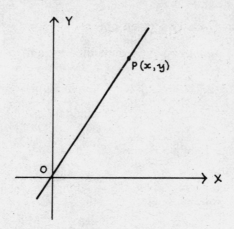

P is a point on the line L distinct from O.

$$L = \{O\} \cup \{P: \text{Mop} = m\}$$
$$= \{O \ (o, o)\} \cup \{P(x, y): \frac{y}{x} = m, x \neq o\}$$
$$= \{(x, y): y = mx\} \quad \text{Since } (o, o) \text{ is the member of this set given}$$
by $x = o$.

Thus $y = mx$ is the equation of the line L.

The equation of the line $y = mx + c$ of the line L through the point $C(o, c)$ with gradient m.

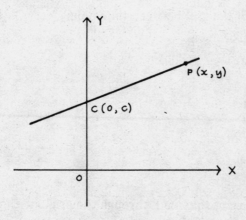

Let $P(x, y)$ be a point on the line L distinct from C.

$$L = \{C\} \cup \{P: \text{Mcp} = m\}$$
$$= \{C \quad (o, c)\} \cup \{P(x, y): \frac{y - c}{x} = m, x \neq o\}$$
$$= \{(x, y): \quad y - c = mx\} \text{ Since } (o, c) \text{ is the member of this set}$$
given by $x = o$.
$$= \{(x, y): \quad y = mx + c\}$$

Thus $y = mx + c$ is the equation of the line L.

The equation of the straight line in the form $y - b = m(x - a)$

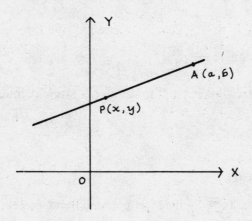

$$L = \{A\} \cup \{P: \quad \text{Map} = m\}$$
$$= \{A(a, b)\} \cup \{P(x, y): \frac{y - b}{x - a} = m, x \neq a\}$$
$$= \{(x, y): y - b = m(x - a)\} \text{ Since } (a, b) \text{ is the member of this}$$
set given by $x = a$.

Thus $y - b = m(x - a)$ is the equation of the line L through the point (a, b) with gradient m.

51

The equation of the form Ax + By + C = 0

$Ax + By + C = 0$ is the equation of a straight line provided A and B are not both zero.

If $A \neq 0$ and $B = 0$ then
$$\{(x, y): Ax + C = 0\} = \left\{(x, y): x = -\frac{C}{A}\right\}$$
which represents a straight line parallel to the y-axis.

If $A \neq 0$ and $B \neq 0$ then
$$\{(x, y): Ax + By + C = 0\} = \left\{(x, y): y = \frac{-A}{B} x + \frac{-C}{B}\right\}$$

$$= \{(x, y): y = mx + c\} \text{ where}$$

$m = \dfrac{-A}{B}$ and $c = \dfrac{-C}{B}$ which is a straight line through the point $\left(0, \dfrac{-C}{B}\right)$ and gradient $\dfrac{-A}{B}$.

Thus $Ax + By + C = 0$ is the equation of a straight line.

Perpendicular Lines

If the line OP with gradient m_1 is perpendicular to the line OQ with gradient m_2, then $m_1 m_2 = -1$.

Proof.   Let OP rotate through $90°$ about 0 so that $P \rightarrow Q$.

If P has co-ordinates (a, b) then under this rotation Q will have co-ordinates $(-b, a)$.

Now $m_1 = \dfrac{b}{a}$ and $m_2 = \dfrac{a}{-b}$ so $m_1 m_2 = \dfrac{b}{a} \times \dfrac{a}{-b}$

$$= -1 \quad [a, b \neq 0]$$

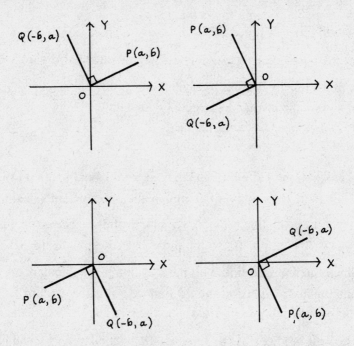

The converse of this theorem is also true i.e. if $m_1\, m_2 = -1$ then OP is perpendicular to OQ. The proof of the converse is given below.

Let OS be a line of gradient m_{OS} which is perpendicular to OP in the plane of OP and OQ.

$m_1\, m_{OS} = -1$ by the theorem and
$m_1\, m_2 = -1$

Hence $m_1\, m_{OS} = m_1\, m_2$
$\Leftrightarrow \qquad m_{OS} = m_2$

Thus OS and OQ are collinear and so OQ is perpendicular to OP.

Finding the equation of a line

To find the equation of a line three pieces of information are necessary:

i)   A point on the line, (a, b) say.

ii) The gradient of the line, m say.

iii) The formula $y - b = m(x - a)$.

Example:

Find the equation of the lines a) parallel and b) perpendicular to the line with equation $2y - 4x = 8$, through the point where $x = 3$.

i)   A point on the line is $(3, y)$. By substitution in the given equation $2y - 4(3) = 8$, $y = 10$, so the point has co-ordinates $(3, 10)$.

ii) Since the required line is a) parallel; b) perpendicular to the given line the given equation should first be put into standard form i.e. $y = mx + c$ i.e. $y = 2x + 4$.

Thus the gradient of the line parallel to the given line will have the same gradient as that line is $m = 2$ and the gradient of the line perpendicular to it will $\dfrac{-1}{m}$ i.e. $\dfrac{-1}{2}$.

iii) The required equations then are by substitution in the formula

a) $y - 10 = 2(x - 3)$ $\Leftrightarrow$ $y = 2x + 4$

b) $y - 10 = -\tfrac{1}{2}(x - 3)$ $\Leftrightarrow$ $y = -\tfrac{1}{2}x + \dfrac{23}{2}$.

The Circle

The equation $x^2 + y^2 = r^2$ describes the locus of a point which is equidistant from the origin.

Let $P(x, y)$ be a point on the locus. Then OP is the distance from the origin i.e. the radius r.

The locus is the set of points $C = \{P(x, y): OP = r\}$.

As is usual with locus problems where the distance formula is involved we square both sides of the equation, thus getting rid of the square root sign in the distance formula i.e.

$$C = \{P(x,y): \quad OP^2 = r^2\}$$
$$= \{(x,y): \quad (x-o)^2 + (y-o)^2 = r^2\}$$
$$= \{(x,y): \quad x^2 + y^2 = r^2\}$$

Note that $x^2 + y^2 < r^2$ describes the area within the circumference of the circle, and $x^2 + y^2 > r^2$ describes the area outside the circumference of the circle.

If the centre of the circle is taken to be the point $A(a, b)$ then the locus of the points equidistant from A and distance r from it describes the circumference of the circle with centre (a, b) and radius r.

Let $P(x, y)$ be a point on the locus.

$$C = \{P(x,y): \quad AP = r\}$$
$$= \{P(x,y): \quad AP^2 = r^2\}$$
$$= \{(x,y): \quad (x-a)^2 + (y-b)^2 = r^2\}$$

By expanding the equation of the circle $(x-a)^2 + (y-b)^2 = r^2$
$$x^2 - 2ax + a^2 + y^2 - 2by + b^2 = r^2$$
$$x^2 + y^2 + 2(-a)x + 2(-b)y + (a^2 + b^2 - r^2) = 0$$
$$x^2 + y^2 + 2(-a)x + 2(-b)y + c = 0$$
$$\text{where } c = (a^2 + b^2 - r^2)$$

Note that the centre has $-(\tfrac{1}{2}$ the coefficient of x) as its x co-ordinate and $-(\tfrac{1}{2}$ the coefficient of y) as its y co-ordinates.

In its more general form the equation of a circle is $x^2 + y^2 + 2gx + 2fy + c = 0$.

This form may be proved to represent a circle of centre $(-g, -f)$ and radius $\sqrt{g^2 + f^2 - c}$.

$\{P(x, y) \;:\; x^2 + y^2 + 2gx + 2fy + c = 0\}$

$\{P(x, y) \;:\; x^2 + 2gx + y^2 + 2fy = -c\}$

Now completing the squares:

$\{P(x, y) \;:\; x^2 + 2gx + g^2 + y^2 + 2fy + f^2 = g^2 + f^2 - c^2\}$

$\{P(x, y) \;:\; (x + g)^2 + (y + f)^2 = g^2 + f^2 - c\}$

$\{P(x, y) \;:\; (x - (-g))^2 + (y - (-f))^2 = g^2 + f^2 - c\}$

$\{P(x, y) \;:\; CP^2 = g^2 + f^2 - c\}$

Where C is the point $(-g, -f)$ i.e. the centre of the circle and $\sqrt{(g^2 + f^2 - c)}$ the distance from the centre to a point $P(x, y)$ on the circumference i.e. the radius, r.

It is important to note that $g, f, c, \in R$ and that $g^2 + f^2 - c \geqslant 0$ because $g^2 + f^2 - c = r^2 \geqslant 0$.

Intersections and Quadratic Forms

A straight line will intersect with a curve whose equation is of quadratic form in

i)   2 points as in the figure below:

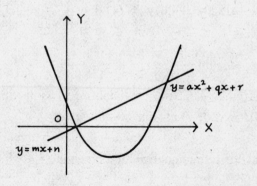

ii) 1 point i.e. when the line is a tangent to the curve as in the figure below:

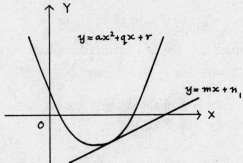

iii) or it will not intersect at all as in the figure below:

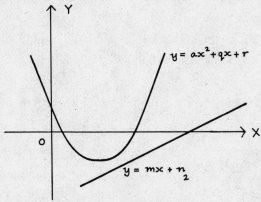

Note that each diagram above assumes the coefficient of x^2 to be positive though it need not be so.

The intersection between the line and the curve may be found by equating the right-hand sides of the equations of the line and the curve e.g.

$$ax^2 + qx + r = mx + n$$

The next step is to solve for x by forming a quadratic equation in its normal form.

$$ax^2 + (q - m)x + (r - n) = 0$$

i.e. $ax^2 + bx + c = 0$

$\Leftrightarrow x = \dfrac{-b \pm \sqrt{b^2 - 4ac}}{2a}$

57

If the discriminant $(b^2 - 4ac) < 0$ then condition (iii) prevails i.e. there is no solution for $x \in R$.

If the discriminant > 0 then condition (i) prevails i.e. there are two points of intersection.

If the discriminant $= 0$ then the straight line is a tangent to the curve at that value of x as in condition (ii).

Example:
Find the points of intersection between the line $y = 3x + 1$ and the parabola $y = 2x^2 + x - 3$.

$$y = 2x^2 + x - 3$$
$$y = 3x + 1 \qquad \Leftrightarrow \quad 2x^2 + x - 3 = 3x + 1$$
$$\Leftrightarrow 2x^2 - 2x - 4 = 0$$
$$\Leftrightarrow x^2 - x - 2 = 0$$
$$\Leftrightarrow (x - 2)(x + 1) = 0$$
$$\Leftrightarrow x = 2 \text{ or } x = -1$$

By substitution in the equation of the line (or the curve) we can find the corresponding values of y.

i.e. $y = 3(2) + 1 = 7$
     $y = 3(-1) + 1 = -2$

i.e. The points of intersection are:
     $(2, 7)$ and $(-1, -2)$.

Compare this section with that on quadratic equations and functions in the algebra section.

Vectors

Internal Division

Given a **line segment** AB and a point, P, on that line segment we say the line is divided in a certain ratio internally by P i.e. P lies between A and B as below:

Here the ratio $\dfrac{AP}{PB} = \dfrac{m}{n}$ and is positive since $\overrightarrow{AP}$ and $\overrightarrow{PB}$ have the same sense.

External Division

Given a **line** AB which of course extends indefinitely beyond A and B as below:

Now a point P can lie on this line either between A and B or outside A and B. If P lies on the line so that P is not between A and B we say the line AB is divided externally in a given ratio as below:

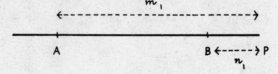

Here the ratio is still $\dfrac{AP}{PB} = \dfrac{m_1}{n_1}$ but is negative since $\overrightarrow{AP}$ and $\overrightarrow{PB}$ have opposite sense.

Now $\dfrac{AP}{PB} = \dfrac{m}{n}$ $\Leftrightarrow$ $\quad n\,AP = m\,PB$

$\Leftrightarrow$ $\quad n\,\overrightarrow{AP} = m\,\overrightarrow{PB}$

$\Leftrightarrow$ $\quad n\,(\overrightarrow{OP} - \overrightarrow{OA}) = m\,(\overrightarrow{OB} - \overrightarrow{OP})$

$\Leftrightarrow$ $\quad n\,(\underline{p} - \underline{a}) = m\,(\underline{b} - \underline{p})$

$\Leftrightarrow$ $\quad n\,\underline{p} - n\,\underline{a} = m\,\underline{b} - m\,\underline{p}$

$\Leftrightarrow$ $\quad n\,\underline{p} + m\,\underline{p} = m\,\underline{b} + n\,\underline{a}$

$\Leftrightarrow$ $\quad (m + n)\,\underline{p} = m\,\underline{b} + n\,\underline{a}$

$\Leftrightarrow$ $\quad \underline{p} = \dfrac{m\,\underline{b} + n\,\underline{a}}{m + n}$

Since $\underline{p} = \begin{pmatrix} x_p \\ y_p \end{pmatrix}$ $\quad \underline{a} = \begin{pmatrix} x_a \\ y_a \end{pmatrix}$ $\quad \underline{b} = \begin{pmatrix} x_b \\ y_b \end{pmatrix}$ then

$$x_p = \frac{mx_b + nx_a}{m + n} \qquad y_p = \frac{my_b + ny_a}{m + n}$$

Thus we may find the co-ordinates of the point of division P, whether it is internal or external, simply by substituting the co-ordinates of A and B.

3D Vectors

If $A\,(2, 3, 4)$, $B\,(5, 7, 9)$ then $\overrightarrow{AB} = \begin{pmatrix} 5 - 2 \\ 7 - 3 \\ 9 - 4 \end{pmatrix} = \begin{pmatrix} 3 \\ 4 \\ 5 \end{pmatrix}$

In general $A\,(x_A, y_A, z_A)$, $B\,(x_B, y_B, z_B)$

$\Leftrightarrow$ $\quad \overrightarrow{AB} = \begin{pmatrix} x_B - x_A \\ y_B - y_A \\ z_B - z_A \end{pmatrix}$

The magnitude of $\overrightarrow{AB}$ above is written $|\overrightarrow{AB}|$

60

i.e.
$$\left| \begin{pmatrix} 3 \\ 4 \\ 5 \end{pmatrix} \right| = \sqrt{3^2 + 4^2 + 5^2}$$

In general $|\overrightarrow{AB}| = \sqrt{(x_B - x_A)^2 + (y_B - y_A)^2 + (z_B - z_A)^2}$

Compare this pattern with that of vectors in two dimension as shown in *Basic Knowledge 'O' Level Mathematics*.

(GRAPE)

If A and B are points in three dimensions i.e. A (x_A, y_A, z_A), B (x_B, y_B, z_B) then the same working holds as for two dimensions only the last line in the proof will be:

$$x_p = \frac{mx_B + ny_A}{m+n} \qquad y_p = \frac{mx_B + ny_A}{m+n} \qquad z_p = \frac{mz_B + nz_A}{m+n}$$

Giving $\overrightarrow{OP} = \begin{pmatrix} x_p \\ y_p \\ z_p \end{pmatrix}$ i.e. P is point (x_p, y_p, z_p).

An alternative method of finding the point which divides a line in a given ratio in 3 dimensions may be seen by the following example.

Find the co-ordinates of P which divides $A(0, -3, -6)$, $B(5, 7, 9)$ in the ratio $2:3$.

Now

$$\vec{AP} = \tfrac{2}{5}\ \vec{AB} = \tfrac{2}{5} \begin{pmatrix} 5 - 0 \\ 7 - (-3) \\ 9 - (-6) \end{pmatrix}$$

$$= \tfrac{2}{5} \begin{pmatrix} 5 \\ 10 \\ 15 \end{pmatrix}$$

$$= \begin{pmatrix} 2 \\ 4 \\ 6 \end{pmatrix}$$

$$\vec{AP} = \vec{OP} - \vec{OA}$$

$$\vec{OP} = \vec{AP} + \vec{OA} = \begin{pmatrix} 2 \\ 4 \\ 6 \end{pmatrix} + \begin{pmatrix} 0 \\ -3 \\ -6 \end{pmatrix} = \begin{pmatrix} 2 \\ 1 \\ 0 \end{pmatrix}$$

Thus P is point $(2, 1, 0)$.

Example:

A B C D is a quadrilateral. P and Q are the mid-points of A B and B C; L and M are the mid-points of D A and D C. Prove that the mid-points of QL and PM are the same point.

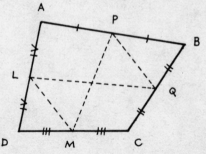

62

Method:

First be sure to draw an adequate figure and mark all information given.

Choose an origin, O say, but do not mark it on the diagram for it will render it too complex to be of value.

Change all line segments to position vector notation e.g. $\overrightarrow{PM}$ becomes $\underline{m} - \underline{p}$, thus we may reduce the geometry problem to one of simple algebra. Now in terms of position vectors list the data given.

$$\underline{p} = \tfrac{1}{2}(\underline{a} + \underline{b}); \quad \underline{q} = \tfrac{1}{2}(\underline{b} + \underline{c}); \quad \underline{l} = \tfrac{1}{2}(\underline{a} + \underline{d}); \quad \underline{m} = \tfrac{1}{2}(\underline{d} + \underline{c})$$

Now we wish to show that the mid-point of PM is the same as the mid-point of QL.

Write down the mid-point of PM, say $\underline{x}_1$

Mid-point of PM, $\underline{x}_1 = \tfrac{1}{2}(\underline{p} + \underline{m})$. Similarly the mid-point of QL, $\underline{x}_2 = \tfrac{1}{2}(\underline{l} + \underline{q})$.

These don't look the same but we can substitute from our given data thus:

$$
\begin{aligned}
\underline{x}_1 &= \tfrac{1}{2}(\underline{p} + \underline{m}) &= \tfrac{1}{2}\left(\tfrac{1}{2}(\underline{a} + \underline{b}) + \tfrac{1}{2}(\underline{d} + \underline{c})\right) \\
&&= \tfrac{1}{4}(\underline{a} + \underline{b} + \underline{c} + \underline{d})
\end{aligned}
$$

$$
\begin{aligned}
\underline{x}_2 &= \tfrac{1}{2}(\underline{l} + \underline{q}) &= \tfrac{1}{2}\left(\tfrac{1}{2}(\underline{a} + \underline{d}) + \tfrac{1}{2}(\underline{b} + \underline{c})\right) \\
&&= \tfrac{1}{4}(\underline{a} + \underline{b} + \underline{c} + \underline{d}) \\
&&= \underline{x}_1.
\end{aligned}
$$

Thus the mid-points are the same.

To show that two line segments are parallel in two dimensions it is sufficient to show that the two line segments may be represented by linear equations with the same gradient e.g. $y = mx + c_1$ and $y = mx + c_2$ are parallel because they both have the same gradient m, as in $y = 3x + 5$ and $y = 3x - 9$.

Example:

Show that the line segments AB and CD are parallel where A(3, 4), B(5, 7) and C(8, −3) and D(12, 3).

Since only the gradients matter:

$$m_{AB} = \frac{y_B - y_A}{x_B - x_A} \qquad m_{CD} = \frac{y_D - y_C}{x_D - x_C}$$

$$= \frac{7 - 4}{5 - 3} \qquad = \frac{3 + 3}{12 - 8}$$

$$= \frac{3}{2} \qquad = \frac{6}{4}$$

$$= \frac{3}{2}$$

Thus $m_{AB} = m_{CD}$ and so the line segment AB and CD are parallel.

However in three dimensions we do not have a formula corresponding to $\frac{y_2 - y_1}{x_2 - x_1}$ but we have a vector equation to assist in the proof i.e.
$\underline{u} = k\underline{v} \Leftrightarrow \underline{u}$ is parallel to $\underline{v}$.

Example:

Show that the line segments AB and CD are parallel where $A(3, 4, 5)$, $B(5, 7, 9)$ and $C(2, -3, 4)$ and $D(6, 3, 12)$.

$$\text{Now } \overrightarrow{AB} = \begin{pmatrix} 5-3 \\ 7-4 \\ 9-5 \end{pmatrix} \qquad \overrightarrow{CD} = \begin{pmatrix} 6-2 \\ 3+3 \\ 12-4 \end{pmatrix}$$

$$= \begin{pmatrix} 2 \\ 3 \\ 4 \end{pmatrix} \qquad = \begin{pmatrix} 4 \\ 6 \\ 8 \end{pmatrix}$$

$$= 2\begin{pmatrix} 2 \\ 3 \\ 4 \end{pmatrix}$$

If we now consider $\overrightarrow{AB}$ to be a representative of $\underline{u}$ and $\overrightarrow{CD}$ a representative of $\underline{v}$ then:

$\overrightarrow{AB} = \frac{1}{2}\overrightarrow{CD} \Leftrightarrow \overrightarrow{AB}$ is parallel to $\overrightarrow{CD}$.

Note that to prove two line segments are collinear i.e. on the same straight line it is sufficient to prove that they are parallel and that there is a common point on both lines.

Example:

Prove that AB and BC are collinear where $A(3, 4, 5)$, $B(5, 7, 9)$, $C(9, 13, 17)$.

$$\overrightarrow{AB} = \begin{pmatrix} 2 \\ 3 \\ 4 \end{pmatrix} \qquad \overrightarrow{BC} = \begin{pmatrix} 4 \\ 6 \\ 8 \end{pmatrix} = 2\begin{pmatrix} 2 \\ 3 \\ 4 \end{pmatrix}$$

i.e. $\overrightarrow{AB} = \frac{1}{2}\overrightarrow{BC} \Leftrightarrow AB$ is parallel to BC and B is a common point thus AB and BC are collinear.

The Scalar Product

Given two points A (x_a, y_a, z_a) and B (x_b, y_b, z_b)

Then $\overrightarrow{OA} = \underline{a} = \begin{pmatrix} x_a \\ y_a \\ z_a \end{pmatrix}$ $\qquad \overrightarrow{OB} = \underline{b} = \begin{pmatrix} x_b \\ y_b \\ z_b \end{pmatrix}$ and

$$\overrightarrow{AB} = \overrightarrow{OB} - \overrightarrow{OA} = \underline{b} - \underline{a} = \begin{pmatrix} x_b - x_a \\ y_b - y_a \\ z_b - z_a \end{pmatrix}$$

$$
\begin{aligned}
|\underline{a}|^2 &= x_a^2 + y_a^2 + z_a^2 \\
|\underline{b}|^2 &= x_b^2 + y_b^2 + z_b^2 \\
|\underline{b} - \underline{a}|^2 &= (x_b - x_a)^2 + (y_b - y_a)^2 + (z_b - z_a)^2
\end{aligned}
$$

Now consider $\triangle$ A O B as in the figure below:

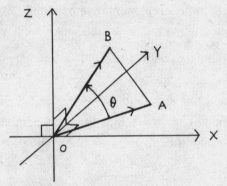

By the cosine rule $AB^2 = OA^2 + OB^2 - 2OAOB\cos\theta$

$$\Leftrightarrow (\underline{b} - \underline{a})^2 = |\underline{a}|^2 + |\underline{b}|^2 - 2|\underline{a}||\underline{b}| \cos\theta$$

From above the formula becomes

L.H.S. $= (x_b - x_a)^2 + (y_b - y_a)^2 + (z_b - z_a)^2$

$= (x_b^2 - 2x_bx_a + x_a^2) + (y_b^2 - 2y_by_a + y_a^2) +$
$(z_b^2 - 2z_bz_a + z_a^2)$

R.H.S. $= (x_a^2 + y_a^2 + z_a^2) + (x_b^2 + y_b^2 + z_b^2) -$
$2\sqrt{(x_a^2 + y_a^2 + z_a^2)(x_b^2 + y_b^2 + z_b^2)} \cos\theta$

By the additive inverse we may remove the terms common to the
R.H.S. and the L.H.S. leaving the equation:

$-2x_ax_b - 2y_ay_b - 2z_az_b = -2\sqrt{(x_a{}^2 + y_a{}^2 + z_a{}^2)(x_b{}^2 + y_b{}^2 + z_b{}^2)}$
$\text{Cos } \theta$

$\Leftrightarrow x_ax_b + y_ay_b + z_az_b = \sqrt{(x_a{}^2 + y_a{}^2 + z_a{}^2)(x_b{}^2 + y_b{}^2 + z_b{}^2)} \text{ Cos } \theta$

$\Leftrightarrow x_ax_b + y_ay_b + z_az_b = |\underline{a}|\,|\underline{b}| \text{ Cos } \theta$

$\qquad\qquad\qquad = \underline{a} \cdot \underline{b}$

Note that θ is the smaller angle required to rotate one vector ($\overrightarrow{OA}$ in the
above diagram) onto another ($\overrightarrow{OB}$ in the above diagram) so that their
sense is the same e.g. in the diagram below the required angle is marked.

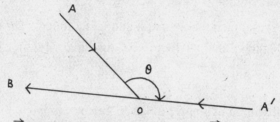

In the diagram $\overrightarrow{OA}$ would have to be rotated to $\overrightarrow{OA^1}$ in order to make
the sense (indicated by the arrow) the same as that of $\overrightarrow{OB}$.

Note that θ lies in the range $0 \leqslant \theta \leqslant \pi$.

If the two vectors concerned are at right angles to each other then:

$\underline{a} \cdot \underline{b} = |\underline{a}|\,|\underline{b}| \text{ Cos } 90°$

$\qquad = |\underline{a}|\,|\underline{b}| \times 0$

$\qquad = 0$

If the two vectors concerned are parallel and have the same sense then:

$\underline{a} \cdot \underline{b} = |\underline{a}|\,|\underline{b}| \text{ Cos } 0°$

$\qquad = |\underline{a}|\,|\underline{b}| \times 1$

$\qquad = |\underline{a}|\,|\underline{b}| \, .$

From which we conclude $\underline{a} \cdot \underline{a} = |\underline{a}|^2$.

Projection

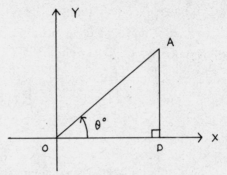

In the figure OD is the projection of OA on the x-axis.

OD = OA Cos $\theta°$.

If $\overrightarrow{OA}$ is a representative of vector $\underline{a}$ and $\underline{u}$ is a unit vector in the direction $\overrightarrow{OX}$ then $|\overrightarrow{OD}|$ = $|\underline{a}.\underline{u}|$ because $\underline{a}.\underline{u} = |\underline{a}||\underline{u}|$ Cos $\theta°$ = OA Cos $\theta°$.

Similarly in the case of the figure given below:

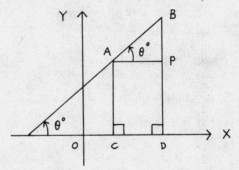

AP = AB Cos $\theta°$ = CD.

If $\overrightarrow{AB}$ is a representative of vector $\underline{a}$ and $\underline{u}$ is a unit vector in the direction $\overrightarrow{OX}$ then $|\overrightarrow{CD}|$ = $|\underline{a}.\underline{u}|$ because $\underline{a}.\underline{u} = |\underline{a}||\underline{u}|$ Cos $\theta°$ = AB Cos $\theta°$.

[Remember $|\underline{u}|$ = 1 since $\underline{u}$ is a unit vector].

The projection $\overrightarrow{CD}$ may be denoted by the symbol p($\underline{a}$).

68

TRIGONOMETRY

Radian Measure

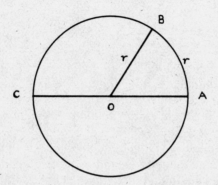

In the diagram the circle with centre 0 has·an arc AB equal in length to the radius, r, of the circle. The circumference of the circle is $2\pi r$.

The length of arc AC where AC is the diameter of the circle is πr.

From the formula the length of an arc depends on the angle $\theta°$ subtended at the centre of the circle i.e. $\dfrac{\theta}{360} \times 2\pi r = l \Leftrightarrow \dfrac{\theta}{180} \times \pi r = l.$

If we now let $l = r$ the formula becomes:

$$\frac{\theta}{180} \times \pi r = r \Leftrightarrow \frac{\theta}{180} \times \pi = 1$$

$$\Leftrightarrow \frac{\theta}{180} = \frac{1}{\pi}$$

$$\Leftrightarrow \pi\theta = 180$$

Now since π is a constant and 180 is a constant the θ must be a constant. This constant θ we will call a radian i.e. $\theta = 1$ radian i.e. the angle subtended at the centre of a circle by an arc equal in length to the radius of that circle is 1 radian. We now have π radians $= 180°$.

Hence $\qquad$ 1 radian $= \dfrac{180°}{\pi} \doteq 57.3°$

$\qquad\qquad\qquad \dfrac{\pi}{2}$ radians $= 90°$

$\qquad\qquad\qquad \dfrac{\pi}{3}$ radians $= 60°$ etc.

Similarly $\qquad \sin (\pi \text{ radians}) \quad = \quad \sin 180°$

$\qquad\qquad\qquad \sin (\dfrac{\pi}{2} \text{ radians}) \quad = \quad \sin 90° \text{ etc.}$

$\qquad\qquad\qquad \cos (x \text{ radians}) \quad = \quad \cos (\dfrac{180x}{\pi})°$

It is unnecessary to write the word 'radians' in such trigonometric functions but simply cos x, sin x, and tan x.

Be sure to distinguish between sin x° (sin (x degrees)) and sin x (sin (x radians)).

Trigonometric Equations

Equations of the form sin x° = k, cos x° = k, and tan x° = k may be solved for x in a given range e.g. $0 \geqslant x < 360$ or $x \in R$ simply by looking up tables and then applying our knowledge of the shape of the graph of the given function e.g.

Sin x° = k may give a value of k = c in the tables, now, by looking at the graph of sin x given below, we see that the sine of many angles will give a value of k.

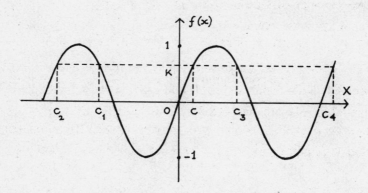

Some of these solutions are marked on the diagram e.g. c, c_1, c_2, c_3, c_4. Because of the periodicity of the sine curve we know that the values of c are related e.g. $c_4 = 360 + c$ and $c_2 = c - 360$. Similarly $c_3 = 180 - c$ and $c_1 = c_3 - 360$. In fact if the diagram were extended in both directions we would find a whole set of solutions all of the form $\{c + n.360\}$ or $\{c_3 + n.360\}$, $n \in Z$.

The general solution then is the union of the two sets $\{(c + n.360)^\circ\}$ $\cup \{(c_3 + n.360)^\circ \quad , n \in Z.\}$

A similar method is adopted for the solution of equations involving $\cos x$ and $\tan x$.

Trigonometric equations may be of a more complex form e.g. $\cos^2 x - 3 \cos x = -2, x \in R.$

As usual we must change the shape of the problem to one we know how to solve. First make one side of the equation zero, giving
$$\cos^2 x - 3 \cos x + 2 = 0$$
$\Leftrightarrow \quad (\cos x - 2) \ (\cos x - 1) = 0$
$\Leftrightarrow \quad \cos x = 2 \ \text{ or } \ \cos x = 1$

Now $\cos x$ cannot equal 2 since the maximum of a cosine is 1, so we find $\cos x = 1$ is our only solution and arises when $x = 0$ or 2π or 4π etc. or $-2\pi, -4\pi$ etc. and in general $x \in \{2n\pi \quad , n \in Z.\}$

The solution then is $\phi \cup \{2n\pi \quad , n \in Z\}$ i.e. $\{2n\pi \quad , n \in Z.\}$

Example:

Find solution set of sin 2x + cos x = 0, $0 \leqslant x \leqslant 2\pi$.

We first change the shape of the equation so as to express the left-hand side as a product of factors. Since 'cos x' is the simplest term we will try to change 'sin 2x' into a form which has cos x as a factor.

$$\sin 2x = 2 \sin x \cos x$$

Thus $\quad \sin 2x + \cos x = 0$

$\Leftrightarrow \quad\quad 2 \sin x \cos x + \cos x = 0$

$\Leftrightarrow \quad\quad \cos x\, (2 \sin x + 1) = 0$

$\Leftrightarrow \quad\quad \cos x = 0$ or $2 \sin x + 1 = 0$

$$\Leftrightarrow \sin x = -\tfrac{1}{2}$$

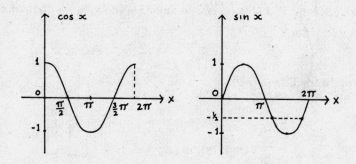

From the graphs we find the solution set to be $\left\{ \dfrac{\pi}{2}, \dfrac{3}{2}\pi, \dfrac{7}{6}\pi, \dfrac{11\pi}{6} \right\}$

The Function a cos x + b sin x

It is often convenient to express a cos x + b sin x in the form k cos (x − α) where k is a positive constant and $0 \leqslant \alpha < 2\pi$.

73

First assume $a \cos x + b \sin x = k \cos (x - \alpha)$

$$= k \cos x \cos \alpha + k \sin x \sin \alpha$$

$$= (k \cos \alpha) \ \cos x + (k \sin \alpha) \sin x.$$

Now by equating coefficients of cos x and sin x on each side we find:

$$k \cos \alpha = a \implies k^2 \cos^2 \alpha = a^2$$

$$k \sin \alpha = b \implies k^2 \sin^2 \alpha = b^2$$

By addition $k^2 \cos^2\alpha + k^2 \sin^2\alpha = a^2 + b^2$

$$\Leftrightarrow k^2 (\cos^2\alpha + \sin^2\alpha) = a^2 + b^2$$

$$\Leftrightarrow k^2 = a^2 + b^2$$

$$\Rightarrow k = \sqrt{(a^2 + b^2)}$$

Also $\dfrac{k \sin \alpha}{k \cos \alpha} = \dfrac{b}{a} \Leftrightarrow \dfrac{\sin \alpha}{\cos \alpha} = \dfrac{b}{a} \Leftrightarrow \tan \alpha = \dfrac{b}{a}$

The quadrant of α (the auxiliary angle) is the same as that of the point $(k \cos \alpha, k \sin \alpha)$ i.e. (a, b).

Formula for Cos $(\alpha + \beta)$

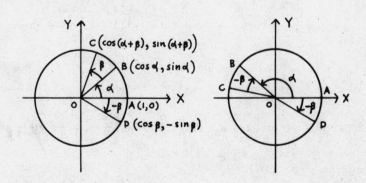

In the diagram $\angle$ AOC $= \alpha + \beta$.

74

Let OC rotate about 0 through $-\beta$ radians so that $A \to D$.

D is the point $(\cos(-\beta), \sin(-\beta))$ i.e. $(\cos\beta, -\sin\beta)$.

Under this rotation $AC \to DB \Leftrightarrow AC = DB \Rightarrow AC^2 = DB^2$.

By the distance formula:

$$
\begin{aligned}
AC^2 &= [\cos(\alpha+\beta) - 1]^2 + [\sin(\alpha+\beta) - 0]^2 \\
&= [\cos^2(\alpha+\beta) - 2\cos(\alpha+\beta) + 1] + [\sin^2(\alpha+\beta)] \\
&= [\cos^2(\alpha+\beta) + \sin^2(\alpha+\beta)] + 1 - 2\cos(\alpha+\beta) \\
&= 1 + 1 - 2\cos(\alpha+\beta) \\
&= 2 - 2\cos(\alpha+\beta).
\end{aligned}
$$

$$
\begin{aligned}
DB^2 &= (\cos\alpha - \cos\beta)^2 + (\sin\alpha + \sin\beta)^2 \\
&= (\cos^2\alpha - 2\cos\alpha\cos\beta + \cos^2\beta) + (\sin^2\alpha + 2\sin\alpha\sin\beta \\
&\quad + \sin^2\beta) \\
&= (\cos^2\alpha + \sin^2\alpha) + (\cos^2\beta + \sin^2\beta) - 2\cos\alpha\cos\beta + \\
&\quad 2\sin\alpha\sin\beta \\
&= 1 + 1 - 2\cos\alpha\cos\beta + 2\sin\alpha\sin\beta \\
&= 2 - 2\cos\alpha\cos\beta + 2\sin\alpha\sin\beta
\end{aligned}
$$

Hence $2 - 2\cos(\alpha+\beta) = 2 - 2\cos\alpha\cos\beta + 2\sin\alpha\sin\beta$

$\Leftrightarrow$ $\cos(\alpha+\beta) = \cos\alpha\cos\beta - \sin\alpha\sin\beta$

Similarly $\cos(\alpha-\beta) = \cos\alpha\cos\beta + \sin\alpha\sin\beta$

Maximum and Minimum Values of a cos x + b sin x

By expressing $a\cos x + b\sin x$ in the form $k\cos(x - \alpha)$ it is readily seen that since the maximum value of a cosine is 1 then the maximum value of $k\cos(x - \alpha)$ is $k.1 = k$.

Similarly the minimum value of a cosine is -1 and so the minimum value of k cos $(x - \alpha)$ is k.$(-1) = -k$.

The value of x for which the maximum and minimum values occur can be found by solving the equations:

$\cos(x - \alpha) = 1$ and
$\cos(x - \alpha) = -1$

for which it is necessary first to evaluate α as in the previous section.

The Equation a cos x + b sin x = c

The equation a cos x + b sin x = c is solved by first converting the L.H.S. to the form k cos $(x - \alpha)$ giving:

$$k \cos(x - \alpha) = c$$

Thus $\cos(x - \alpha) = \dfrac{c}{k}$ which can be solved in the usual way.

Example:

Solve the equation 3 cos x° + 4 sin x° = 5 for $0 \leqslant x < 360$.

$$
\begin{aligned}
\text{Let } 3 \cos x° + 4 \sin x° &= k \cos(x - \alpha)° \\
&= k \cos x° \cos \alpha° + k \sin x° \sin \alpha°
\end{aligned}
$$

Thus
$$k \cos \alpha° = 3 \qquad\qquad \tan \alpha° = \tfrac{4}{3} = 1.33$$
$$k \sin \alpha° = 4 \qquad\qquad \alpha° = 53.1°$$
$$k = \sqrt{3^2 + 4^2} = 5$$

Thus $5 \cos(x - 53.1)° = 5$
$\Leftrightarrow \quad \cos(x - 53.1)° = 1$
$\Leftrightarrow \quad (x - 53.1)° = 0°$
$\Leftrightarrow \quad x = 53.1$

Calculus

1. Differentiation

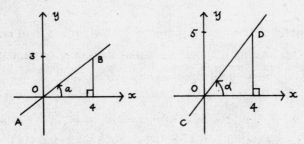

Line AB has equation $y = \frac{3}{4} x \Leftrightarrow \frac{y}{x} = \frac{3}{4} \Leftrightarrow \tan a = \frac{3}{4}$

Line CD has equation $y = \frac{5}{4} x \Leftrightarrow \frac{y}{x} = \frac{5}{4} \Leftrightarrow \tan \alpha = \frac{5}{4}$

The ratio found from these equations gives the value of the tangent of the angle the lines make with the positive direction of the x-axis i.e. the gradients of the lines. The gradient tells us by how many units y changes as x changes e.g. for line AB y changes by 3 units for every 4 that x changes. The ratio then tells us the rate of change in y with respect to x i.e. the gradient (m) tells us the rate of change in y with respect to x.

Since $\frac{y - y_1}{x - x_1} = m = \tan \theta$, then $\frac{y - y_1}{x - x_1}$ represents the rate of change in y with respect to x.

This rate of change is the derivative of the function under consideration. The function represented by the line AB is f(x) = ¾ x. The derivative of this function is written as f'(x) and in this case f'(x) = ¾. In the case of line CD, f'(x) = $\frac{5}{4}$.

The derivative of a function which is represented by a straight line is a constant i.e. its gradient is constant.

The gradient of a line $f(x) = \frac{3}{4}x + c$ is the same as that of $f(x) = \frac{3}{4}x$ because the lines are parallel and so the rate of change is the same for both lines i.e. $f'(x) = \frac{3}{4}$.

The constant 'c' in the function does not affect the rate of change. This is only reasonable from the fact that lines may be parallel although the constant c_1 may be different in any given cases.

Consider too $f(x) = c$. This function is represented by a straight line parallel to the x axis, so that $f'(x)$ does not change i.e. $f(x) = c \Leftrightarrow f'(x) = 0$.

Now consider the case where $f(x)$ is not a function represented by a straight line, as in the figure below.

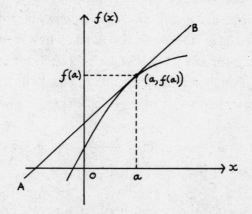

Here the rate of change of $f(x)$ with respect to x is not constant.

As is usual in mathematics we try to reduce a complex problem to a simple one which we know how to do. In the above case we make a straight line, in fact we can make as many straight lines as there are points on the graph of the function.

78

First we choose a point on the graph at which we wish to know the rate of change, say $(a, f(a))$. Now consider the tangent to the curve at that point i.e. AB. The gradient of this tangent is taken to be the rate of change of $f(x)$ with respect to x at that point. By our usual method of finding the gradient i.e.

$\dfrac{f(x) - f(a)}{x - a}$ which corresponds to $\dfrac{y_2 - y_1}{x_2 - x_1}$

However we do not have any values for $f(x)$ and x to use as replacements. We therefore choose a point which is so close to $(a, f(a))$ as not to alter the true value of the gradient i.e. we choose $((a + h), f(a + h))$ where h is as near the value zero as is necessary for our purpose. The gradient then becomes:

$\dfrac{f(a + h) - f(a)}{(a + h) - a} = \dfrac{f(a + h) - f(a)}{h}$

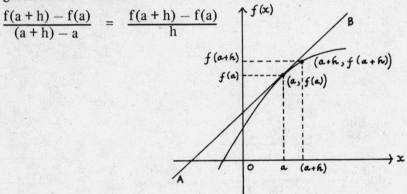

Now by taking the limit (see algebra section) of this ratio as $h \to 0$ (h tends to zero) we have the required value of the gradient or $f'(a)$ i.e.

$f'(a) = \underset{h \to 0}{\text{Lim}} \dfrac{f(a + h) - f(a)}{h}$ and in general

$f'(x) = \underset{h \to 0}{\text{Lim}} \dfrac{f(x + h) - f(x)}{h}$

If we use this ratio to evaluate $f'(x)$ we say we have found the derivative from first principles.

79

Example:

Find the derivative of $f(x) = 2x + 3$ from first principles.

$f(x) = 2x + 3$ $\qquad$ $f(x + h) = 2(x + h) + 3$

$$
\begin{aligned}
f'(x) &= \lim_{h \to 0} \frac{f(x+h) - f(x)}{h} \\
&= \lim_{h \to 0} \frac{[2(x+h) + 3] - [2x + 3]}{h} \\
&= \lim_{h \to 0} \frac{2x + 2h + 3 - 2x - 3}{h} \\
&= \lim_{h \to 0} \frac{2h}{h} \\
&= 2
\end{aligned}
$$

Notice again that 2 is the gradient of the line $f(x) = 2x + 3$.

Example:

Differentiate from first principals $f(x) = \dfrac{1}{x^2}$.

$$
f(x) = \frac{1}{x^2}
$$

$$
\begin{aligned}
f'(x) &= \lim_{h \to o} \frac{f(x+h) - f(x)}{h} \\
&= \lim_{h \to o} \frac{\dfrac{1}{(x+h)^2} - \dfrac{1}{x^2}}{h} \\
&= \lim_{h \to o} \frac{\dfrac{x^2 - (x+h)^2}{x^2 (x+h)^2}}{h} \\
&= \lim_{h \to o} \frac{x^2 - x^2 - 2hx - h^2}{x^2 (x+h)^2 \, h} \\
&= \lim_{h \to o} \frac{-h (2x + h)}{x^2 (x+h)^2 \, h} \\
&= \lim_{h \to o} \frac{-1 (h + 2x)}{x^2 (x+h)^2}
\end{aligned}
$$

[Note as $h \to o$, $(x + h)^2 \to (x + o)^2 = x^2$]

$$
\begin{aligned}
&= \frac{-2x}{x^4} \\
&= \frac{-2}{x^3}
\end{aligned}
$$

By considering the expansion of $(x + h)^n$ we arrive at a quick method of finding $f'(x)$ when $f(x) = x^n$.

$$(x + h)^2 = x^2 + 2xh + h^2 \qquad\qquad = x^2 + 2xh + h^2$$
$$(x + h)^3 = x^3 + 3x^2h + 3xh^2 + h^3 \qquad = x^3 + 3x^2h + h^2(3x + h)$$
$$(x + h)^4 = x^4 + 4x^3h + 6x^2h^2 + 4xh^3 + h^4 = x^4 + 4x^3h + h^2(6x + 4xh + h^2)$$
$$(x + h)^n = x^n + nx^{n-1}h + h^2 \text{ (Some expression in x)}$$

Thus $\displaystyle \lim_{h \to o} \frac{f(x + h)^n - x^n}{h} = \lim_{h \to o} \frac{x^n + nx^{n-1}h + h^2(-----) - x^n}{h}$

$$= \lim_{h \to o} \frac{nx^{n-1}h + h^2(-------)}{h}$$

$$= nx^{n-1}$$

By multiplying all the above by a constant c then $f'(x) = cnx^{n-1}$ when $f(x) = cx^n$.

The rule then is that if $f(x) = x^n$, $f'(x) = nx^{n-1}$ for all $n \in Z$ unless $x = 0$ when n is negative (which would give an undefined form $\frac{k}{0}$)

Note that if $f(x) = x^{-n}$ then by the quick method $f'(x) = -nx^{-n-1} = \dfrac{-n}{x^{n+1}}$ but when $x = o$, $\dfrac{-n}{o^{n+1}}$ is undefined.

Increasing and Decreasing Intervals

When a tangent at a point on the graph of a function makes an acute angle with the positive direction of the x-axis we say the function is increasing at that point.

When the angle is obtuse we say the function is decreasing at that point.

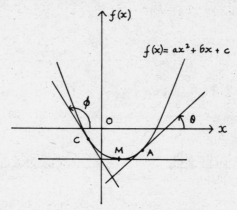

In short, a function is increasing at any point where the gradient of the tangent at that point is positive, because the tangent of an acute angle is positive. A function is decreasing at any point where the gradient of the tangent at that point is negative, because the tangent of an obtuse angle is negative.

Since f′ (x) is the gradient of a tangent we can write the above statements in symbols.

f′ (x) > o ⇔ f (x) is increasing
f′ (x) < o ⇔ f (x) is decreasing

We are left now with the case where f′ (x) = o i.e. at the point M in the above diagram. Notice that the tangent at M, the minimum value of f (x) in this case, is parallel to the x-axis and so the angle between the tangent and the x-axis is o°.

At the minimum (or maximum) value of a function the tangent is parallel to the x-axis and so the gradient of the tangent at that point is zero i.e. f′ (x) = o.

At the maximum or minimum value of a function the rate of change is neither increasing nor decreasing and is said then to be stationary.

Compare the above with the movement of a stone thrown into the air. The stone is increasing in its height above the ground till it reaches its maximum height, then it must become stationary before it starts to fall when its height above the ground will decrease.

When the maximum or minimum value of a function has been found we are dealing with a maximum or minimum stationary value, or a maximum or minimum turning value.

All turning or stationary values need not be the maxima or minima of functions e.g. consider a bouncing ball whose path is illustrated by the following diagram.

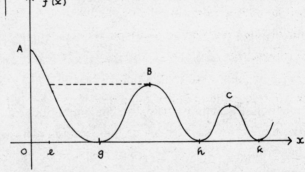

Here A is the maximum height of the ball. B and C show the maximum heights reached after each bounce. The tangents to the curve at these points are parallel to the x-axis, and so there are stationary values at B and C.

We could say that B was the maximum value in the interval [g, h] i.e. the closed interval, meaning the end points are included, $g \leqslant x \leqslant h$. Similarly C is the maximum value in the interval [h, k]. Even if we increase the interval to [e, k] notice that B is still the maximum turning point.

Such maxima and minima are not the only types of stationary values in a function. Consider a rocket fired into the air whose second stage is fired just as the first stage reaches its maximum height. This might be depicted as the following graph.

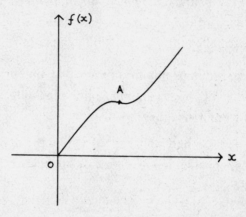

At the point A the rocket ceases to rise from the first stage boost but just as the thrust ends the second stage fires and causes the rocket to rise further. Such a stationary point is called a point of inflexion.

Notice that at a point of inflexion the graph does not change from an increasing to a decreasing part of the function but that it increases up to the stationary value at the point of inflexion and then continues to increase from there.

A point of inflexion can occur when a function decreases then tapers off to a stationary value then decreases again.

All points of inflexion need not be stationary values but only those whose tangent at that point is parallel to the x-axis i.e. when $f'(x) = 0$.

Despite these complications regarding stationary values the test is very simple, for such values are easily located by considering for which values of x is $f'(x) = 0$.

Having located the stationary values the problem of determining what kind they are remains. However by considering what happens to the function just before and just after the stationary value we find a simple solution to the problem.

Minimum

If $f'(x) = o$ when $x = a$

	a^-	a	a^+
$f'(x)$	$-$	o	$+$
	$\searrow$	$\rightarrow$	$\nearrow$

Maximum

If $f'(x) = o$ when $x = a$

	a^-	a	a^+
$f'(x)$	$+$	o	$-$
	$\nearrow$	$\rightarrow$	$\searrow$

Points of Inflexion

If $f'(x) = o$ when $x = a$

	a^-	a	$a+$
$f'(x)$	$-$	o	$-$
	$\searrow$	$\rightarrow$	$\searrow$

	a^-	a	a^+
$f'(x)$	$+$	o	$+$
	$\nearrow$	$\rightarrow$	$\nearrow$

Example.

Find the stationary values of the function f defined by $f(x) = x^2 (x-1)^2$ and determine their nature. Sketch the graph of the function.

$$
\begin{aligned}
f(x) &= x^2 (x-1)^2 \\
&= x^2 (x^2 - 2x + 1) \\
&= x^4 - 2x^3 + x^2
\end{aligned}
$$

$$
\begin{aligned}
f'(x) &= 4x^3 - 6x^2 + 2x \\
&= 2x (2x^2 - 3x + 1) \\
&= 2x (2x - 1)(x - 1)
\end{aligned}
$$

$f'(x) = 0$ when $x = 0$ or $x = \frac{1}{2}$ or $x = 1$

x	0^-	0	0^+
2x	−	o	+
(2x − 1)	−	−	−
(x − 1)	−	−	−
$f^1(x)$	−	o	+
	↘	→	↗

Minimum Stationary
(0, 0)

x	$\frac{1}{2}^-$	$\frac{1}{2}$	$\frac{1}{2}^+$
2x	+	+	+
(2x − 1)	−	o	+
(x − 1)	−	−	−
$f^1(x)$	+	o	−
	↗	→	↘

Maximum Stationary
$(\frac{1}{2}, \frac{1}{16})$

x	1^-	1	1^+
2x	+	+	+
(2x − 1)	+	+	+
(x − 1)	−	o	+
$f^1(x)$	−	o	+
	↘	→	↗

Minimum Stationary
(1, 0)

When $x = 0$, $f(0) = 0$ so graph goes through the origin.

When $f(x) = 0$, $x^2 (x - 1)^2 = 0 \Leftrightarrow x = 0$ or $x = 1$.

When x is a large positive value f(x) is large and positive.

When x is a large negative value f(x) is large and positive.

86

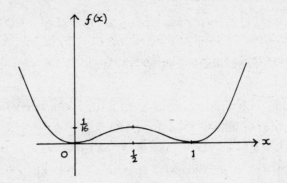

Note that when f(x) has a factor which is a square then the x-axis will be a tangent to the curve at the value of x which makes that factor zero as for $x = 0$ and $x = 1$ above from the factors x^2 and $(x - 1)^2$ respectively.

Example.
Determine the interval for which the function $f(x) = \frac{1}{3} x^3 - x^2 - 3x + 3$
is a) increasing b) decreasing

$f'(x) = x^2 - 2x - 3$
$\qquad = (x + 1)(x - 3)$

Here it is advisable to sketch the curve of $f'(x)$ which is NOT the same as the curve $f(x)$.

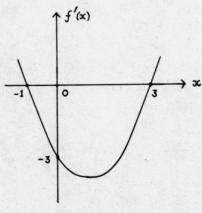

The function f (x) is increasing when f' (x) > 0 i.e. − 1 > x or x > 3.

The function f (x) is decreasing when f' (x) < 0 i.e. − 1 < x < 3.

When dealing with a closed interval of a function then the maximum or minimum value need not be a stationary value of the function e.g. in the diagram below the maximum value of the function is at f(a), and the minimum at f(b), if we deal with the closed interval [a, b].

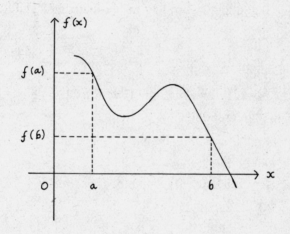

It should be realised that not all functions are differentiable. A function, f, is differentiable when the domain of f is the domain of f'.

Note that before attempting to find $f'(x)$ we should, if possible, express $f(x)$ as a sum or difference of terms and then differentiate each term individually.

Note also if $y = f(x)$ then $f'(x)$ may be written as $\dfrac{dy}{dx}$ or $\dfrac{df}{dx}$.

Example.
Find the maximum and minimum values of $f: x \to 2x - x^2$ in $[-1, \frac{3}{2}]$. Sketch the graph.

$$
\begin{aligned}
f(x) &= 2x - x^2 \\
f'(x) &= 2 - 2x \\
&= 2(1 - x) = 0 \Leftrightarrow x = 1.
\end{aligned}
$$

Thus the only stationary value is:
$$
\begin{aligned}
f(1) &= 2(1) - (1)^2 \\
&= 1.
\end{aligned}
$$

This value lies in the given interval.

x	1^-	1	1^+
$1 - x$	+	0	−
$f'(x) = 2(1 - x)$	+	0	−
	↗	→	↘

Thus $x = 1$ gives a maximum stationary value of $f(1) = 1$.

The values of f at the end points of the interval $[-1, \frac{3}{2}]$ are $f(-1) = -3$ and $f(\frac{3}{2}) = \frac{3}{4}$.

Thus the minimum value in the interval is -3.

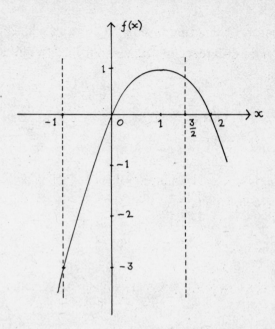

Thus $-3 \leqslant f(x) \leqslant 1$.

Notice that the maximum and minimum values asked for are those of the function i.e. $f(x)$ not the values of x.

Example.

Find the equation of the tangent to the curve $f(x) = x^2 + 3$ at the point where $x = 2$.

i) The point on the line is $(2, f(2))$. By substitution in the given function $f(2) = 2^2 + 3 = 7$ so the point is $(2, 7)$.

ii) The gradient $m = f'(x) = 2x \Rightarrow f'(2) = 2.2 = 4$.

iii) The required equation by substitution in the form
$y - b = m(x - a)$ is $y - 7 = 4(x - 2) \Leftrightarrow y = 4x - 1$.

90

Example.

Find the equation of the tangent(s) to the curve $f(x) = x^3 - 3x^2 - 3x + 2$ whose gradient is 6.

$$f(x) = x^3 - 3x^2 - 3x + 2$$
$$f'(x) = 3x^2 - 6x - 3$$

Since $\quad f'(x) = m = 6$ then

$$3x^2 - 6x - 3 = 6$$
$$\Leftrightarrow \quad 3x^2 - 6x - 9 = 0$$
$$\Leftrightarrow \quad 3(x^2 - 2x - 3) = 0$$
$$\Leftrightarrow \quad 3(x + 1)(x - 3) = 0$$
$$\Leftrightarrow \quad x = -1 \text{ or } x = 3$$

$\Leftrightarrow \quad$ The tangents of gradient 6 occur at $x = -1$ and $x = 3$.

Now when $x = -1 \ f(-1) = 1$
and when $x = 3 \ f(3) = -7$
i.e. $m = 6$ at points $(-1, 1)$ and $(3, -7)$.

The equation of the tangents at these points are:
$y - 1 = 6(x + 1)$ and $y + 7 = 6(x - 3)$
$\Leftrightarrow y = 6x + 7$ and $y = 6x - 25$.

Further Differentiation

1. $(f(x))^n$ e.g. $(ax^3 + bx^2 + cx + d)^n$

Method: Treat the bracket as a single variable X and differentiate as usual, giving $n(ax^3 + bx^2 + cx + d)^{n-1}$. Now differentiate what is inside the bracket i.e. $(3ax^2 + 2bx + c)$ then take the product of the two results giving $n(3ax^2 + 2bx + c)(ax^3 + bx^2 + cx + d)^{n-1}$.

2. $\dfrac{1}{\sqrt{f(x)}}$ e.g. $\dfrac{1}{\sqrt{(ax^2 + bx + c)}}$

Method: Express in a form without the root sign i.e.
$(ax^2 + bx + c)^{-\frac{1}{2}}$. Now proceed as in 1 above.
$-\frac{1}{2}(2\,ax + b)\,(ax^2 + bx + c)^{-\frac{3}{2}}$.

3. Sin (f(x)) e.g. sin (5x + 2).

Method: Treat the bracket as a single variable X and differentiate as usual, giving cos (5x + 2). Now differentiate what is inside the bracket i.e. 5 then take the product of the two results giving 5 cos (5x + 2).

4. $\cos^n x$

Method: Consider the expression in the form $(\cos x)^n$. Now as before treat the bracket as a single variable X and differentiate giving $n\,(\cos x)^{\,n-1}$. Now differentiate inside the bracket giving $-\sin x$, then find the product of the two results i.e. $-n \sin x \cos^{n-1} x$.

Integration

Integration may be considered as the inverse operation of differentiation. For example to differentiate the form x^n the following steps were taken:

1. Subtract the constant.
2. Multiply x^n by the index.
3. Subtract 1 from the index.

The inverse of this for integration of x^n.

1. Add 1 to the index.
2. Divide x^{n+1} by the index.
3. Add a constant.

Thus
$$\int x^n dx = \frac{x^{n+1}}{n+1} + C.$$

An exception to this rule is when $n = -1$ for then
$$\int x^{-1} dx = \frac{x^{-1+1}}{-1+1} + C = \frac{1}{0} + C \text{ but the form } \frac{1}{0} \text{ is undefined.}$$

Notes

1. $\int f(x)\, dx$ is called the indefinite integral i.e. when no limits are given. In such a case a constant of integration must be added e.g. $\int x^2\, dx = \dfrac{x^3}{3} + C$. The value of 'C' is not known without further information.

2. $\int kf(x)\, dx = k\int f(x)\, dx$, where k is any constant.

3. $\int [f(x) + g(x)]\, dx = \int f(x)\, dx + \int g(x)\, dx$.

4. $\int_a^b f(x)\, dx + \int_b^c f(x)\, dx = \int_a^c f(x)\, dx$.

5. $\int_a^b f(x)\, dx = -\int_b^a f(x)\, dx$.

When limits of integration are involved we are dealing with a definite integral e.g. $\int_1^2 x^n dx$. Here the '1' is the lower limit and the '2' the upper limit of integration.

$$\int_1^2 x^n dx = \left[\frac{x^{n+1}}{n+1}\right]_1^2$$

$$= \left[\frac{2^{n+1}}{n+1}\right] - \left[\frac{1^{n+1}}{n+1}\right]$$

$$= \frac{2^{n+1} - 1}{n+1}$$

Note that no constant of integration is required when dealing with a definite integral.

Before attempting to integrate any function it is advisable to ensure that it is in the form of a sum or difference of terms each of the shape

93

ax^n e.g.

$$\int \frac{(x^2 + x)^2}{x} \, dx = \int \frac{x^4 + 2x^3 + x^2}{x} \, dx$$

$$= \int \left(\frac{x^4}{x} + \frac{2x^3}{x} + \frac{x^2}{x} \right) dx$$

$$= \int (x^3 + 2x^2 + x) \, dx$$

$$= \frac{x^4}{4} + \frac{2x^3}{3} + \frac{x^2}{2} + C.$$

Integration may be used to find the area between a curve, the x-axis and the lines x = a and x = b. If the function is f(x) then we would write $\int_a^b f(x) \, dx$ to refer to the above area. The diagram illustrates this.

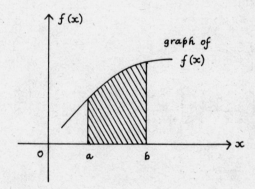

graph of f(x)

Cautions

1. When integrating a single function to find the area between the curve and the x-axis, first check whether for any values between the given limits the curve crosses the x-axis.

94

e.g.

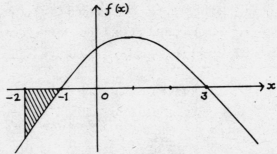

In the figure the shaded area is below the x-axis and so the value of f(x) will be negative. If then it is necessary to find the area between the curve the x-axis and x = −2 and x = 3 i.e. $\int_{-2}^{3} f(x)\,dx$ we should split the integral into two parts viz. $\int_{-2}^{-1} f(x)\,dx$ and $\int_{-1}^{3} f(x)\,dx$ and on evaluation sum the magnitudes of the integrals.

2. If the area between two curves is involved there is no need to worry about the crossing of the x-axis. If a negative answer arises it simply means that the functions have been dealt with in the reverse order and so we use the magnitude of this result, e.g. to find the area between f(x) and g(x):−

a) If possible make a sketch.

b) Find the points of intersection.

c) Use these points as limits, say a and b.

d) Evaluate $\int_{a}^{b} [f(x) - g(x)]\,dx$, where g(x) would be the lower curve of the sketch over the enclosed area.

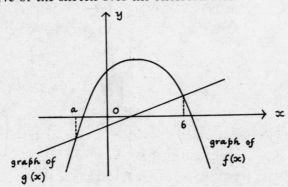

95

3. Note the difference between being asked to a) evaluate $\int_0^2 (x^3 - 3x^2 + 2x)\, dx$ and b) find the area between the curve $x^3 - 3x^2 + 2x$ and the x-axis from x = 0 to x = 2.

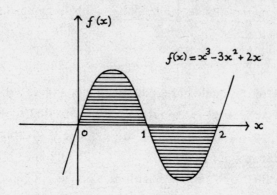

The answer to (a) is 0, but obviously, from the sketch the area asked for is the shaded region, which is not 0.

a) $\int_0^2 (x^3 - 3x^2 + 2x)\, dx$ $= \left[\dfrac{x^4}{4} - x^3 + x^2 \right]_0^2$

$= \dfrac{16}{4} - 8 + 4 - 0$

$= 0$

b) $\int_0^2 (x^3 - 3x^2 + 2x)\, dx$ $= \int_0^1 (x^3 - 3x^2 + 2x)\, dx +$
$\left| \int_1^2 (x^3 - 3x^2 + 2x)\, dx \right|$

$= \left[\dfrac{x^4}{4} - x^3 + x^2 \right]_0^1 +$
$\left| \left[\dfrac{x^4}{4} - x^3 + x^2 \right]_1^2 \right|$

$= \left[\dfrac{1}{4} - 1 + 1 \right] - 0 + \left| \left[\dfrac{16}{4} - 8 + 4 \right] \right.$
$\left. - \left[\dfrac{1}{4} - 1 + 1 \right] \right|$

$= \dfrac{1}{4} + \left| \left[0 - \dfrac{1}{4} \right] \right| = \dfrac{1}{4} + \dfrac{1}{4} = \dfrac{1}{2} \text{ units}^2.$

Volumes of Revolution

The volume of a cylinder is given by the formula $\pi r^2 h$ so we use this fact to calculate the volume generated by rotating a section of area about an axis. The method is to break the area into strips and then rotate the strips to form cylinders and finally add the volumes of the cylinders.

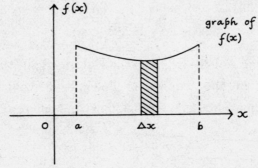

In the figure above the value of r, for the cylinder generated by rotating the shaded strip, is the height of the curve above the x-axis i.e. f(x) and similarly for all the other cylinders we want to form. The value of h for each cylinder is Δx which in the limit will be dx, so $\pi r^2 h$ becomes for our purposes $\pi(f(x))^2$ dx.

The sum of these in the limit will be denoted by $\int_a^b \pi(f(x))^2$ dx or more conveniently $\pi \int_a^b (f(x))^2$ dx or even more conveniently $\pi \int_a^b y^2$ dx.

We could use the same system in rotating an area about the y-axis. The formula for such a system is found simply by interchanging the x and the y i.e. $\pi \int_c^d x^2$ dy.

Note that when we use dx we are rotating about the x-axis and so the limits (a and b) come from the x-axis, but when we use dy we are rotating about the y-axis and so the limits (c and d) come from the y-axis.

We may generate a solid of revolution by rotating the area between two curves about an axis. The formula for this is $\pi \int_a^b ([f(x)]^2 - [g(x)]^2)\, dx$, where $f(x)$ and $g(x)$ represent the two curves. All we are doing here is finding the volume generated by rotating $f(x)$ which is the outside of a hollow cylinder and then subtracting the volume of the inside of the cylinder which is generated by rotating $g(x)$.

Example.

Find the area of the region in the first quadrant which is bounded by the line $y = x$ and the curve $y = x^3$. Find also the volume of the solid formed by rotation of this area through one complete revolution about the x-axis.

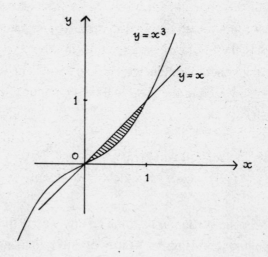

The required area is shaded in the above diagram. The curves intersect in the first quadrant when $x = 0$ and when $x = 1$.

$$A = \int_0^1 (x - x^3)\, dx$$
$$= [\tfrac{1}{2} x^2 - \tfrac{1}{4} x^4\,]\,\Big|_0^1 = \tfrac{1}{2} - \tfrac{1}{4} = \tfrac{1}{4} \text{ units}^2$$

$$V = \pi \int_0^1 [(x)^2 - (x^3)^2]\, dx$$
$$= \pi \int_0^1 (x^2 - x^6)\, dx$$
$$= \pi [\tfrac{1}{3} x^3 - \tfrac{1}{7} x^7]\,\Big|_0^1$$
$$= \pi [\tfrac{1}{3} - \tfrac{1}{7}]$$
$$= \tfrac{4}{21} \pi \text{ units}^3$$

Further Integration

1. The form $(ax + b)^n$

   Method: Guess the integral then differentiate this result and compare with the original expression. From here we may readily see what extra factors are required. Note that any bracket in the integrand will probably appear in the integral.

   $\int (ax + b)^n dx$

   Guess: $\dfrac{(ax + b)^{n+1}}{n+1} + C$

   Differentiate the guess: $\dfrac{(n+1)(ax+b)^n a}{n+1} = (ax + b)^n a$

   We have an extra factor 'a' so divide the guess by 'a' i.e.

   $\dfrac{(ax + b)^{n+1}}{a(n+1)} + C$.

2. The form $\int \sin(ax + b)\, dx$.

   Guess: $\cos(ax + b) + C$.

   Differentiate the guess: $[-\sin(ax + b)]\, a$.

   Divide the guess by the extra factor '$-a$' giving $\dfrac{-\cos(ax + b)}{a} + C$.

99

The following conventions and formulae should be known for the Examination in Mathematics, Higher Grade.

Areas and Volumes

1. Curved surface area of cylinder, base radius r, height h $= 2\pi rh$.
2. Volume of cylinder $= \pi r^2 h$.
3. Curved surface area of cone base radius r, slant height s $= \pi rs$.
4. Volume of cone base radius r, height h $= \frac{1}{3}\pi r^2 h$.
5. Surface area of a sphere of radius r $= 4\pi r^2$.
6. Volume of a sphere of radius r $= \frac{4}{3}\pi r^3$.

Algebra

Sets

1. $A \subset B$, i.e. A is a subset of B, if for all $x \in A$, $x \in B$.
2. The complement of a set A with respect to a universal set $\&$ is denoted by A'.
3. The following conventions for naming sets will be used. N is the set of natural numbers (positive integers). Z is the set of integers. Q is the set of rational numbers. R is the set of real numbers.
4. Subsets of R can be represented as segments of the number line. The end points are indicated by circles, shaded if the end points are included, open if the end points are excluded e.g.

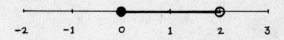

5. Subsets of $\{(x, y): x \in R, y \in R\}$ can be represented as areas on a cartesian diagram. If points on the boundary lines are included the line should be continuous otherwise it should be broken.

6. If an operator $*$ is defined on a set A with elements a_1, a_2, a_3 ...... then in the operation table for that operator the entry in the ith row and jth column is $a_i * a_j$.

Functions

1. If a function, f, has domain A, the values of $f(x)$, $x \in A$ constitute the range of the function.

2. If f is a function from B into C and g is a function from A into B then $f \circ g$ is a function from A into C such that $f \circ g(x) = f(g(x))$ for all $x \in A$.

3. If a function f is one-one and onto it has an inverse function denoted by f^{-1}.

Quadratic Function

1. The roots of $ax^2 + bx + c = 0$ are $\dfrac{-b \pm \sqrt{(b^2 - 4ac)}}{2a}$ $a \neq 0$

2. If α, β are the roots of $ax^2 + bx + c = 0$ then $\alpha + \beta = \dfrac{-b}{a}$, $\alpha\beta = \dfrac{c}{a}$.

Logarithms

$$\text{Log}_b a = \frac{\log_c a}{\log_c b}$$

Series

1. Sum of n terms of the standard arithmetic series is $\dfrac{n}{2}(2a + (n-1)d)$.

2. Sum of n terms of the standard geometric series is $\dfrac{a(1 - r^n)}{1 - r}$ $r \neq 1$.

3. "Sum to infinity" of the standard geometric series is $\dfrac{a}{1-r}$, $-1 < r < 1$.

Matrices

The matrix $A = \begin{pmatrix} a & b \\ c & d \end{pmatrix}$ has inverse $A^{-1} =$

$$\begin{pmatrix} \dfrac{d}{ad-bc} & \dfrac{-b}{ad-bc} \\[3mm] \dfrac{-c}{ad-bc} & \dfrac{a}{ad-bc} \end{pmatrix}$$ provided $ad - bc \neq 0$.

Scalar Product

1. $\underline{a}.\underline{b} = |\underline{a}||\underline{b}| \cos\theta$ where θ is the angle between $\underline{a}$ and $\underline{b}$
2. $\underline{a}.\underline{b} = a_x b_x + a_y b_y + a_z b_z$ where a_x, a_y, a_z and b_x, b_y, b_z are the components of $\underline{a}$ and $\underline{b}$ respectively in three mutually perpendicular directions.

Geometry

1. The translation $\begin{pmatrix} a \\ b \end{pmatrix}$ maps the point (x, y) onto the point $(x + a, y + b)$.
2. A dilatation $[A, k]$ maps the point P onto the point P^1 such that $\overrightarrow{AP^1} = k \overrightarrow{AP}$.
3. If m_1, m_2 are the gradients of two lines then $m_1\ m_2 = -1 \Leftrightarrow$ the lines are perpendicular.
4. The equation $x^2 + y^2 + 2gx + 2fy + 2fy + c = 0$ represents a circle centre $(-g, -f)$ radius $\sqrt{(g^2 + f^2 - c)}$ provided $g^2 + f^2 - c \geqslant 0$.
5. If $\underline{a}$ is the position vector of A and $\underline{b}$ is the position vector of B, then C, the point dividing AB in the ratio $m:n$ has position vector $\underline{c} = \dfrac{1}{m+n}(m\underline{b} + n\underline{a})$

Trigonometry

1. Sine rule $\dfrac{a}{\sin A} = \dfrac{b}{\sin B} = \dfrac{c}{\sin C}$

2. Cosine rule $a^2 = b^2 + c^2 - 2\,bc\cos A$.

3. Area of a triangle $= \frac{1}{2}\,bc\sin A$.

4. Table of exact values of sine, cosine and tangent of certain angles.

	0°	30°	45°	60°	90°
sin	0	$\dfrac{1}{2}$	$\dfrac{1}{\sqrt{2}}$	$\dfrac{\sqrt{3}}{2}$	1
cos	1	$\dfrac{\sqrt{3}}{2}$	$\dfrac{1}{\sqrt{2}}$	$\dfrac{1}{2}$	0
tan	0	$\dfrac{1}{\sqrt{3}}$	1	$\sqrt{3}$	–

5. $\sin(A \pm B) = \sin A \cos B \pm \cos A \sin B$.

6. $\cos(A \pm B) = \cos A \cos B \mp \sin A \sin B$.

7. $\tan(A \pm B) = \dfrac{\tan A \pm \tan B}{1 \pm \tan A \tan B}$

8. $\cos 2A = \cos^2 A - \sin^2 A = 2\cos^2 A - 1 = 1 - 2\sin^2 A$.

9. $\sin 2A = 2\sin A \cos A$.

10. $\tan 2A = \dfrac{2\tan A}{1 - \tan^2 A}$

11. $\cos^2 A = \frac{1}{2}(1 + \cos 2A)$, $\sin^2 A = \frac{1}{2}(1 - \cos 2A)$

12. $2\sin A \cos B = \sin(A + B) + \sin(A - B)$.

13. $2\cos A \cos B = \cos(A + B) + \cos(A - B)$.

14. $2\sin A \sin B = \cos(A - B) - \cos(A + B)$.

15. $\sin A + \sin B = 2\sin\dfrac{A + B}{2}\cos\dfrac{A - B}{2}$

16. $\sin A - \sin B = 2 \cos \dfrac{A + B}{2} \sin \dfrac{A - B}{2}$

17. $\cos A + \cos B = 2 \cos \dfrac{A + B}{2} \cos \dfrac{A - B}{2}$

18. $\cos A - \cos B = 2 \sin \dfrac{A + B}{2} \sin \dfrac{B - A}{2}$

$= -2 \sin \dfrac{A+B}{2} \sin \dfrac{B-A}{2}$

Calculus

1. If $\dfrac{f(x + h) - f(x)}{h}$ tends to a limit as $h \to o$, f is differentiable at x. The limit is the derivative of f at x written $f'(x)$.

f(x)	f'(x)	
x^n	$n x^{n-1}$	
$\sin x$	$\cos x$	where x is in circular measure
$\cos x$	$-\sin x$	

2. $\dfrac{d}{dx} f(g(x)) = f'(g(x)) \, g'(x)$

3.

f(x)	$\int f(x)\,dx$	
x^n	$\dfrac{1}{n + 1} x^{n+1}$ $n \neq -1$	
$\sin x$	$-\cos x$	where x is in circular measure
$\cos x$	$\sin x$	

4. $\int f(ax + b)\,dx = \dfrac{1}{a} F(ax + b)$ where $F(x) = \int f(x)\,dx$.

5. The area bounded by $y = f(x)$ the x-axis and the lines $x = a$ and $x = b$ is $\int_a^b (f(x))\,dx$.

The volume of the solid of revolution obtained by rotating the above area through 2π radians about the x-axis is $\pi \int_a^b (f(x))^2\,dx$.